Great
Maritime
Museums
of the
World

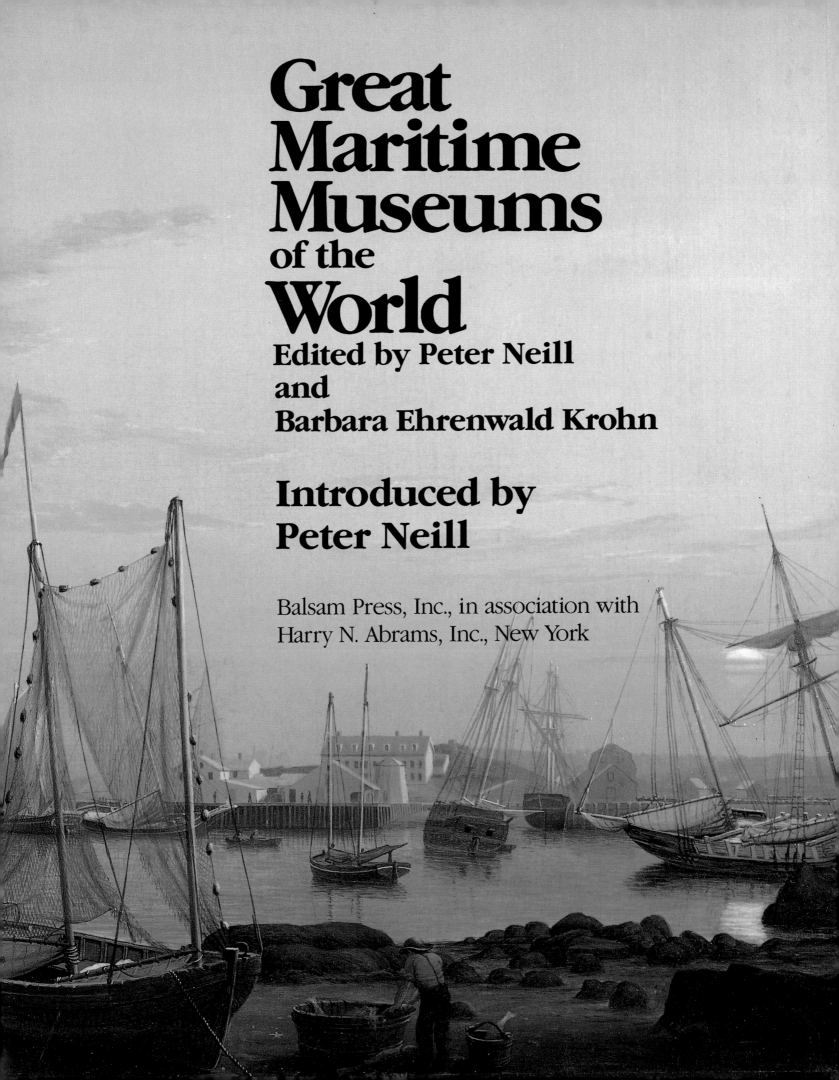

Great Maritime Museums

of the

World

**Edited by Peter Neill
and
Barbara Ehrenwald Krohn**

**Introduced by
Peter Neill**

Balsam Press, Inc., in association with
Harry N. Abrams, Inc., New York

Page 1: *This model of the American-built* Flying Cloud *was made in 1851 by Charles Carlson of Liverpool who used the knowledge he acquired serving as carpenter on many sailing ships to build an extremely accurate model. One of the fastest sailing ships ever built,* Flying Cloud *made the hazardous journey from New York to San Francisco, via Cape Horn, in 89 days. (Courtesy of The Board of Trustees of the National Museums and Galleries on Merseyside, Liverpool, United Kingdom)*

Pages 2-3: Gloucester Inner Harbor, *by Fitz Hugh Lane (1804-65) is both an accurate depiction of the artist's hometown as well as a superb example of luminism, an artistic approach that used soft light to unify the works of man and nature. (Courtesy of The Mariners' Museum, Newport News, Virginia, United States)*

Right: *Using anthropomorphic or zoomorphic figures to decorate the ends of ships is a maritime tradition of great antiquity, dating back at least 3,500 years. Three 19th-century female figureheads that once adorned the bows of American or possibly British ships now welcome visitors into the Smithsonian's Hall of American Maritime Enterprise. (Photo by Eric Long, courtesy of the Smithsonian Institution, Washington, D.C., United States)*

Following pages: Toulon, Site of the Artillery Park, *by Claude-Joseph Vernet, one of the 15 views of French harbors painted by this consummate draughtsman between 1754 and 1765. The series is one of the most famous testimonies on maritime life in the second half of the 18th century. (Courtesy of the Musée de la Marine)*

Editors' Note:
    The photographs in each chapter are reproduced courtesy of the respective museums unless otherwise indicated.
    This anthology is composed of contributions from thirteen countries each of which was permitted to use its own spelling conventions. This was done not only to be tactful but also to furnish at least a verbal hint of local color. A certain number of literal translations have been preserved in this same spirit. We hope that what we may have lost in consistency, we will have gained in individuality.
    Finally, our appreciation goes out to the myriad curators, directors, photo editors, translators, and other staff members of the worldwide network of maritime museums whose cooperation allowed this complex project to bear fruit. Their patience and generosity have been a model of international cooperation.

Published by Balsam Press, Inc.
1 Madison Avenue, New York, New York 10010
in association with Harry N. Abrams, Inc., New York
A Times Mirror Company
Manufactured in Hong Kong by Mandarin Offset
Designed by Allan Mogel
Production by Layla Productions, Inc.

Library of Congress Cataloging-in-Publication Data

Great maritime museums of the world / edited by Peter Neill and Barbara Ehrenwald Krohn : introduction by Peter Neill.
       p.   cm.
       Includes index.
    Summary: Curators from twenty-four of the world's greatest maritime museums describe the historical and geographic significance of the art and artifacts of their collections.
    ISBN 0-8109-3362-4 (Abrams)—ISBN 0-917439-12-0 (Balsam)
    1. Naval museums—Juvenile literature. [1. Naval museums.
2. Museums.] I. Neill, Peter. 1941–   . II. Krohn, Barbara Ehrenwald.
1935–
V13.A1074   1991
387'.0074—dc20
                                              91-10432
                                                   CIP
                                                    AC

CONTENTS

Introduction:

THE UNIVERSAL SHORE

by Peter Neill

The identity of a nation is defined by its geography, language, and art—where it is, what it says about itself, what it makes. These characteristics are unique and manifest themselves in the detail of each nation's social and political history. The rise and fall of nations is a kind of terrestrial tide, an ebb and flow that encompasses the achievements of heroes and tyrants like the flotsam and jetsam in a succession of breaking waves.

Museums reflect this tide and, indeed, each of the museums contained herein looks inward to the evolution of a national history. The artifacts in these collections—whether the simplest tool or the most ornate treasure—evoke a specific event or reflect the skill of an individual hand. As objects, they are art; as art, they are the language of a people, of a community settled on some distant shore.

But what strikes me most forcibly as I leaf through these pages is not the separateness, but the commonality of cultures as disparate geographically as North American and Australian or Scandinavian and Japanese. What accounts for this is the fact that these are maritime museums, which must also look outward, over the sea, to a horizon that ends at yet another landfall, another port of call, another language, another culture. The inevitable exchange has, over time, revealed common experience, discovered new ideas, and transcended the insularity of nations.

I can identify no fewer than eight themes woven together here like a sailor's piece of fancy ropework. The reader will, no doubt, perceive more. And from this sampling it is hoped the reader will commence an even longer voyage (aboard a ship!) to visit these extraordinary places and to discover the full depth of these collections and the full breadth of maritime history ranged along a universal shore.

Opposite: *One of a pair of superb early 18th-century brass and alloy terrestrial and celestial globes attributed to Thomas Wright, who was one of a small circle of high precision instrument-makers operating in the Fleet Street district of London. (Courtesy of the National Maritime Museum, Greenwich, United Kingdom)*

FISHING AND FARMING

Our first theme is found in indigenous seaside culture, typically based on fishing and saltwater farming as a source of sustenance—the Norwegian coast, for example, or the Chesapeake Bay in the United States, or the banks fishery of the Canadian Maritime Provinces. The Norsk Sjøfartsmuseum, Oslo, Norway, contains an exemplary exhibit on this subject, as does the Mariners' Museum, Newport News, Virginia, United States. The Maritime Museum of the Atlantic, Halifax, and the Fisheries Museum, Lunenburg, Nova Scotia, Canada, are a brilliant partnership in their interpretation of the cycles of living relative to the rhythms of season and sea. These original native expressions remain alive today in the commercial fishing fleet of Norway's Lofoten Islands, the skipjacks dredging oysters under sail in Maryland waters, or the large number of working watermen who still ply the rocky coast of Nova Scotia.

The artifacts associated with these traditions also reflect their reliance on small craft and gear, just as they reveal the importance of the marine harvest in religion, poetry, and song. And the museums follow. Sensing the imminent loss of a critical piece of regional culture, the Musée du Bateau in Douarnenez, France, has laid plans for a "living harbor" in which historic ships and replicas will find a communal home. And the Musée de la Pêche in Concarneau, France, has oriented its exhibits around fish species, relating boat type, gear, and net design to artifacts evocative of local folk traditions; the vitality of this culture is palpable.

VOYAGES OF EXPLORATION

A second theme focuses on voyages of exploration, the great sea voyages that delineated our world. And here we begin to see the interrelation of collections and exhibits.

The boats of the Viking Ship Museum in Roskilde, Denmark, are breathtaking in their grace and beauty and intimidating in their seeming vulnerability to the challenges of an ocean passage. And yet these open boats have proved to be among the most seaworthy of vessel design, their success evidenced by the remains of Nordic settlements found in Greenland and sites on the North American shore. Associate these Atlantic vessels with their Pacific counterparts—the comparably fragile outrigger canoes of Polynesia that form the centerpiece of the exhibits at the Hawaii Maritime Museum, Honolulu, Hawaii, United States—and one's sense of the courage and seamanship required to make such journeys is extended into a second hemisphere.

Other voyages are equally illustrative. While material from the 1938 Wilkes expedition to the Pacific and Antarctica forms an important element in the collections of the Smithsonian Institution, Washington, D.C., United States, artifacts associated with Christopher Columbus are predictably found in the Barcelona Maritime Museum, Barcelona, Spain, and those of Captain James Cook are found in the National Maritime Museum, Greenwich, England; the Australian National Maritime Museum, Sydney, Australia; and the Vancouver Maritime Museum, Vancouver, British Columbia, Canada.

MARITIME TECHNOLOGY

A third theme relates the history of maritime technology. The extraordinary models on display in the Nederlands Scheepvaart Museum, Amsterdam, the Netherlands, are a fascinating catalog of the evolution of ship type, hull form, and rig. The Admirality models in the National Maritime Museum, Greenwich, or the National Watercraft Collection, in the Smithsonian Institution, Washington, D.C., or the Crabtree Collection in the Mariners' Museum, Newport News, are similar in quality. As all of these vessels are lost and most are undocumented by plans or drawings, these models are our only source of precious information about early ship construction and operation.

In some instances, of course, the ships do remain in various forms of preservation. One of the earliest and most interesting is a 14th-century Baltic cog that has been recovered through nautical archaeology and is on display in a conservation tank inside the Deutsches Schiffahrtsmuseum, Bremerhaven, West Germany. This museum also keeps other large historic ships, as do, among others, the United States's Mystic Seaport Museum, Mystic, Connecticut; South Street Seaport Museum, New York, New York; and San Francisco Maritime National Historical Park, San Francisco, California. The decision to accept the responsibility for the care and restoration of these highly endangered examples of maritime heritage is problematic. The cost is tremendous, the task formidable, but nothing is more directly evocative of the story to be told than the actual ship that made the history.

Two of the most successful and dramatic examples of ship conservation and restoration are the *Vasa*, National Maritime Museums, Stockholm, Sweden, and the S. S. *Great Britain*, S. S. *Great Britain* Project, Bristol, England. In 1628, on her maiden voyage, the man-of-war *Vasa* capsized in Stockholm harbor, "sails and flags flying," having been hit by a sudden gust of wind that heeled the ship over until water flooded through her open gun ports. While this ignominious event is no tribute to either technology or seamanship, her recovery in 1961 is. The waterlogged wood was treated with new chemicals to displace moisture, and then some 12,000 pieces of the ship were repositioned. The scale and detail of the ship's construction are awe inspiring. No more so, however, than the *Great Britain,* by contrast an iron ship and powered by a steam engine turning a screw propellor. Built in 1844, the *Great Britain* went into passenger service to New York and to Australia, serving thirty-two years until, no longer economically competitive, she was stripped of her engines and reduced to sailing coal from South Wales to San Francisco. Damaged off Cape Horn, her abandoned hulk was used as a floating warehouse in the Falkland Islands. Incredibly, efforts to return her to Bristol were successful, and her restoration has preserved one of the world's most important ships and a mighty symbol of the Industrial Revolution.

NAVIGATIONAL SCIENCE

A fourth theme concerns navigational science. The Museu de Marinha, Lisbon, Portugal; the Nederlands Scheepvaart Museum, Amsterdam; and the National Maritime Museum, Greenwich, possess brilliant collections of early maps and instruments that document the evolution of seafarers' attempts to locate themselves on the changing, challenging surface of the sea. The sextants and compasses, astrolabes and timepieces, are objects of great beauty, finely crafted in their own right and suggestive in their precision of the mathematical "order" discovered by science in the movement of the planets. We take such things for granted now, the ability to sight the sun and to place a mark upon the chart, "Our ship is here."

NAVAL WARFARE

A fifth theme concerns naval warfare, the devastating battles fought far from land that changed the course of many a conflict and frequently realigned the balance of power. England and Spain were great sea forces, and the defeat of the Spanish Armada was such an historic encounter. The Musée de la Marine, Paris, France, has wonderful paintings of the French fleet in full engagement, just as the Mariners' Museum, Newport News, has the artifacts recovered from the wreck of the ironclad *Monitor* off the North Carolina coast, where she foundered after her inconclusive battle with the Confederate ship *Virginia* (ex-*Merrimac*). The permanent exhibit of the Australian National Maritime Museum, Sydney, celebrates the visit of the American "great white fleet" to the Pacific. The San Francisco Maritime National Historical Park, San Francisco, has, in association with its collection, the fully restored Liberty ship *Jeremiah O'Brian,* one of the few remaining such vessels mass-produced dur-

Above: *By 1844, the hull of Col. John Stevens's steamboat* Little Juliana *had deteriorated beyond repair. Accordingly, the original steam engine and boiler underwent a minor overhaul and were installed in a new boat which was exhibited at New York in October, 1844. During trials in the Hudson River, the small craft attained a speed of eight miles per hour. It was then placed on exhibition in New Jersey before being transplanted into a new hull in time for the Columbian Exposition. In new trials nearly 90 years after its construction, it reached the same speed. (Photo by Eric Long, courtesy of the Smithsonian Institution)*

Left: *Lithographs like this one one from 1910 were used in advertisements in Japan for the first time in 1900. This poster for the Nippon Yusen Kaisha (NYK) line dates to the earliest years when kimono-clad beauties of that time were featured with ships in the background. The parasol is imprinted with "NYK" and information about the voyage appears above it. (Courtesy of the Yokohama Maritime Museum, Yokohama, Japan)*

Below: *A 17th-century wooden sculpture of a man's head placed in the mouth of a dog, symbolizing watchfulness. This type of wood carving was often placed on top of the rudder of Dutch inland craft. (Courtesy of the Nederlands Scheepvaart Museum, Amsterdam, Netherlands)*

Left: *This lifejacket, which consists of blocks of cork, came from the White Star liner,* Titanic, *that sank on her maiden voyage from Southampton to New York on April 15, 1912, after hitting an iceberg. Nearly 1,500 of the more than 2,200 passengers and crew perished. The lifejacket was recovered by a member of the crew of the Cunarder RMS* Carpathia *(1903) which was the first rescue ship to appear at the scene of the disaster. (Courtesy of The Board of Trustees of the National Museums and Galleries on Merseyside)*

ing World War II and the backbone of the Allied merchant marine supply effort worldwide.

PORTS AND TRADE

Indeed, throughout history, ships were the purveyors of goods, locally, along the coast, and internationally. The first ports became centers of finance and, as trade flourished, grew into the world's great cities. Thus, our sixth theme, ports and trade, is predictably the focus of the South Street Seaport Museum, New York and the Yokohama Maritime Museum, Yokohama, Japan, two centers that remain strong in contemporary international exchange. The cities of San Francisco and Vancouver traded coastwise, primarily lumber, as well as internationally for spice and tea with India and China; their maritime museums, both "museums of the Pacific Rim," reflect this similar story in the thousands of historic photographs contained in their collections.

The exhibits of the Prins Hendrik Maritime Museum, Rotterdam, the Netherlands, epitomize, physically and historically, the confluence of factors that create a great port city. At the center of its orientation display is a spectacular model of the port facilities wherein can be seen the full spectrum of 19th-century port activity: fisheries, ship construction, inland distribution of goods, and oceanic trade. A most fortuitous contrast can be made between this view of the old port and the contemporary port, one of the world's busiest, with literally thousands of ship movements daily—large freighters, river barges, fishing boats, tugs, dredges, and myriad other service vessels. This traffic is controlled by a sophisticated radar system ranging from the ocean upriver; indeed, managed with the skill associated with a busy airport.

MIGRATION

While ports were functionally concerned with the shipment of production, we should not forget that through them passed millions of people—port workers, seamen, emigrants, and immigrants. These last carried their humble baggage of ideas, customs, individual talents, and experience that constituted yet another kind of invaluable exchange. Among the museums that have addressed this seventh theme of migration, the Merseyside Maritime Museum, Liverpool, England, stands out. The museum has devoted a large portion of its wonderfully renovated historic building at Prince Albert Dock to an evocation of the emigrant/immigrant experience: the decision to seek another opportunity, the hardship of passage in the 'tween deck of a ship, and the arrival and reality of building a new life in a new land. The exhibit attempts to recreate the stages of this journey, specifically immigration from Liverpool to New York, and succeeds with sometimes uncanny similitude.

THE COMMUNITY OF THE SEA

Commonality of experience builds community, and the community of the sea is the eighth theme, best represented here by the Mystic Seaport, Mystic. No other museum has succeeded so well in demonstrating the atmosphere of maritime life. Devoted to the history of "New England and the sea," Mystic has assembled a "village" of historic buildings associated with such marine skills and trades as fishing and oystering, boatbuilding, sail making, coopering, rope making, and blacksmithing. Alongside these, however, stand the captain's house, the sailors' home, the schoolhouse, the apothecary shop, the printer's shop, the general store, and the village tavern. On Mystic's streets and cobblestone wharves, the whaling ship *Charles W. Morgan,* the fishing schooner *L. A. Dunton*, and a vast array of indigenous small craft evoke the atmosphere and pace of life in a small New England coastal village.

Museums can sometimes be perceived as mausoleums, but there is no danger of that here. The vitality of these institutions is undeniable, evident in the artifacts themselves and in the interpretative programs that each museum delivers to its public. Moreover, these museums are responsible for much of the scholarly research in maritime history today, the publications, and the educational innovations that have made them such successful contributors to their national cultural identity.

These and hundreds of other maritime museums worldwide are mirrors of a renewed interest in things maritime that is apparent in almost every nation. Port cities are rediscovering their waterfronts as places to work and to live and to celebrate their heritage. Gatherings of "tall ships," maritime festivals, and regattas draw tremendous audiences, and the water continues to offer opportunity for recreation in boats, small and large.

Just as important are the innumerable manifestations of maritime activity that exist outside museum walls. I seek them out whenever and wherever I can. I think of the feluccas on the Nile, the steam vessels on Lake Geneva, the ferryboats on the Bosphorus in Istanbul, the hydrofoils to Macao, the water taxis in Venice, or the excursion boats cruising through the spectacular scenery of the Rhine or the Yangtse rivers. I think of the sardine fishery in Peniche, Portugal, the salmon fishery in Washington State, the weirs and shore-based nets of the fishermen of Goa or the Philippines, the fish tugs in Two Rivers, Wisconsin. I think of the Fulton Fish Market, the Tsukiji Market in Tokyo, the Bombay market in India. I think of the ship-breaking yard in Kaoshiung, Taiwan, the sunken American fleet in Pearl Harbor, and the hulks of clipper ships in the Falkland Islands' Port Stanley. I think of the live-aboard communities in Hong Kong, Bangkok, Seattle, and Sausalito. I think of the icebreakers and corracles, of Mindinao canoes and modern sea kayaks, of J boats and E scows, of canal barges, windjammers, and cruise lines. I think of locks and drydocks, ropewalks and chain forges, lighthouses and lifesaving stations, of floating prisons and bathhouses, floating oil rigs, bridges, and tunnels. My mind is awash.

But, ultimately, I think of all the fine, honest people I have met who are associated with the sea. I am inspired by their simplicity, energy, and individualism. It is a privilege to work among them, and I dedicate this book to them, curators all, as keepers of a culture that is universal.

THE AUSTRALIAN NATIONAL MARITIME MUSEUM, SYDNEY

by Jeffrey Mellefont, Manager, Public Affairs

A ustralia has been called the world's largest island, or the island continent. This huge landmass, its coastline stretching 36,735 kilometres—not much less than the earth's circumference—is entirely bounded by oceans. Its nearest neighbors are the islands of South East Asia and Oceania. Its front door is the vast Pacific Ocean. It is whole oceans distant from the Old and New Worlds. This is the geographical reality that has determined much of Australia's human history, and it is why so much of that history is maritime history.

Australians now have a new National Maritime Museum to represent all the maritime experiences of inhabiting a country that their national anthem calls a "land girt by sea." The Australian National Maritime Museum is the country's newest museum, but it may represent the world's oldest continuous maritime history.

Not once in the succession of ice ages since human beings have lived on earth has Australia been joined to another continent by a land bridge. The first settling of Australia— believed to have occurred 40,000 to 50,000 years ago—required the use of watercraft of unknown design to bridge the straits between South East Asia and the southern land. Rafts of bamboo have been suggested.

For much of the ensuing millennia, those surrounding oceans allowed Australia's Aborigines to develop their complex cultures undisturbed by the waves of migrations and invasions that were peopling and repeopling the Old and New Worlds. The majority of Aborigines lived close to those same seas and developed rich maritime cultures. Their artistic expressions of this continuing relationship with the sea are as much a feature of the Australian National Maritime Museum's aboriginal displays as their artifacts and watercraft.

Mariners and their historians know that, ultimately, oceans are far more highways than barriers. Thus, it is surprising how long Australia hid in the southern seas. The vast Malayo-Polynesian migratory voyages of recent millennia, which started just to the north of Australia and encompassed the oceans to the west and east—from East Africa to Easter

Opposite: *Australia's first towns were ports channeling goods, people, and information among the new colonies, the interior, and overseas. Today, every state capital and virtually every major Australian city is built around a port. This J. R. Ashton engraving of Circular Quay, ca. 1886, shows Sydney's oldest waterfront entering its second century.*

Island—either missed Australia altogether or left no traces on it.

Trade routes of the old maritime cultures of Asian and Arab worlds came close to the north of Australia, but no more than a hint of its existence is to be found in their skimpy annals. Not until three or four centuries ago did one modest trade—in the unattractive sea cucumber, or *bêche-de-mer*—bring Asian mariners to the island continent's northern littoral. The museum's lateen-rigged Indonesian *lete-lete*, a large, oceangoing *bêche-de-mer* trader, is a contemporary link with this pre-European industry.

When Europeans ventured at last onto the great maritime stages of the Indian and Pacific oceans, they were intent on the wealth of spices in the Indies close to the north of Australia. They gave Australia the most perfunctory of glances and largely ignored it for a century and a half—except if they were wrecked upon its low coasts because of the failure of their reckoning of latitude.

Charts and globes in the museum collection show a variety of names for the southern land: Terra Australis, New Holland, Van Diemen's Land. Two centuries separated the first cartographer's partial sketch and the final inking in of a continuous coastline by the man—Matthew Flinders—who gave it its final name: Australia. Flinders came from the British culture that at about the time of the American Revolution had possessed the maritime resources as well as the desire to colonize the island continent on the opposite side of the world.

The isolation imposed by oceans would continue to shape the history, the economy, and to an extent not always recognized by the people themselves, the hopes, fears, and aspirations that made up the identity of those now called Australians. One of Australia's most eminent historians has termed the net effect of this geographical circumstance "the tyranny of distance."

In 1787-88, 1,030 convicts, jailers, and a naval governor in eleven ships sailed 24,241 kilometres in 250 days to establish a prison settlement in southeastern Australia. This was a single flotilla of migration whose distance, scale, and logistics were unheard of in European affairs. Then, when the largely chartered fleet sailed back to England, the political and sociological peculiarities of the experiment immediately asserted themselves on the colony's maritime history. Totally dependent on the sea for survival, the colonists were forbidden to build boats larger than fourteen feet on the keel both to keep the convicts from escaping and to protect the British East India Company's monopoly on Far Eastern trade.

Even so, the colony's first industries were the maritime ones of whaling and sealing, and the port of Sydney where the National Maritime Museum is located drew much of its early prosperity from servicing the international fleets of whalers—American, French, British—that roamed the Pacific during the early 19th century.

As the balance of population shifted from Aboriginal to British and wider European ancestry, the isolation by sea was compounded by the sense of vast distance from the wellsprings of each arriving group's culture. Until the very recent decades of jet travel, those

Opposite, top: *Journalists from the Melbourne newspaper* The Argus *row to gather world news carried by the newly arrived American-built clipper ships* Red Jacket *and* James Baines *in Hobson's Bay, Victoria. Oil on canvas by Thomas Robertson, ca. 1857. The clippers' faster passages helped to ease Australia's isolation, and record sailing times made headlines.*

Opposite, bottom left: *Australians, largely coastal dwellers, have incorporated a culture of recreation by the seaside into their national makeup. These art deco murals painted for a surf lifesaving club reflect changing beach fashions and the emergence of strong role models in the manly lifesaver and the languid beach beauty. Oil on board by D. H. Souter, 1934. (On loan from Bondi Surf Bathers Lifesaving Club)*

Opposite, bottom right: *Australia's often stormy industrial relations with its maritime workers—seamen and dockers—reflect the country's total dependence on ports and seaways for vital imports and exports. This turn-of-the-century trade union banner was painted by Edgar Whitbread.*

who traveled to Australia to make a new home did so by sea, and the distance was underlined by every day of the longest voyage of their lives.

This is also true of the most recent wave of seaborne migration to Australia, that of Indo-Chinese refugees fleeing their homes during the late 1970s in overcrowded, ill-equipped fishing boats on voyages brought to life at the Australian National Maritime Museum. For the "boat people," however, the sheer distance of ocean separating them from their new home was less than the dangers and hardships of attempting the voyage at all.

The first settlements in Australia (port towns that are now the major cities and state capitals) could be as isolated from one another as they were from foreign countries, such was the size of this largely arid land that is sparsely populated to this day. The sea remained the essential highway for internal communications until well into this century, with the advent of effective roads and long-distance trucking.

River transport also helped defeat this tyranny of distance in the southeast states, opening up inland areas for settlement and agriculture. There were no *Mississippi Queens*, just rough little side-wheelers for snag-strewn rivers that dried up to puddles in the summer.

Not until recent decades was coastal shipping eclipsed by land transport around Australia's arid northwest, where the roads remained rough bush tracks until a few years ago. It was on this unique frontier, where the outback comes down to the ocean and tropical seas

wash desert coasts, that Australia's pearling industry flourished over the last century. Little port towns like Broome combined the legends of the outback with those of the rough pearl-diver's trade, and combine them still with modern trades like offshore oil drilling. Pearling luggers like the museum's *John Louis*, acquired at the end of its working life in 1987, were part of the country's last fleet of commercial sail.

For a variety of historical reasons, Australians have rarely controlled the overseas shipping services on which they rely for their imports and exports. This has made their economic relationship with the sea ambivalent, for the cost of shipping is often subtracted from their standard of living. The colorful history of Australian labor relations has whole maritime chapters, with the most turbulence often found where seamen or waterside workers control the vital points of import or export supply lines.

A country with an ocean on every border is rarely content to substitute distance for naval defenses. When, like Australia, its population and resources are too small to support the navy its long coastline requires, the doings of the great powers' navies in nearby oceans become a matter of immense concern. At the same time, its naval victories in various wars become matters of great national pride. World War II's Battle of the Coral Sea, in which Australians participated in the U.S. Navy's defeat of a Japanese fleet, is remembered each year in Australia with ceremony and relief. Together with the destruction of British battleships in the earlier fall of Singapore, it changed Australia's strategic perceptions and set new alliances on a course for the next half century.

Australians have such a profound reputation for enjoying themselves that they sometimes wonder whether they are unabashed hedonists. Nowhere can this be seen more clearly than in the great national love affair with the water. Blessed by temperate to tropical weather, Australians flock to oceans, rivers, lakes, pools, and dams to relax and to compete, to swim, surf, ski, race anything that floats, and very often just to lie in the sun and turn browner and browner. The figures on the beach, whether bathing beauty, bronzed lifesaver, or body surfer, have provided whole generations with images of themselves that have entered the culture and become part of the national identity. Sporting victories, like a cluster of swimming gold medals or the winning of the 1983 America's Cup, can bring the nation to a standstill.

The new Australian National Maritime Museum is unusual among the country's national museums and galleries in being the only one located outside the national capital, Canberra. However, its place in Sydney, the nation's oldest European settlement and port, is unarguable—and it is unarguably one of the great maritime museum sites in the world. Located at Darling Harbour, an arm of Sydney Harbour adjoining the central business district, the museum is at once part of the working port and part of an ambitious new urban renewal scheme that has created a major waterfront recreational area.

The museum building, with its soaring steel-and-glass exhibition halls and the wharves for its varied collection of historical Australian vessels, has already become a Sydney landmark. Many have noted in its roofline the tribute paid by its architect, Philip Cox,

Opposite: *Figurehead of the 126-gun three-decker HMS* Nelson, *the largest ever English line-of-battle ship when launched in 1814. In 1867, it became a training ship for the colonial navy of the Australian State of Victoria. The carving of Admiral Horatio Nelson has been extensively restored after many years of exposure to the weather in naval shore facilities.*

Above: *Death mask of Commodore James Graham Goodenough, killed in 1875 by a poisoned arrow while cruising the Solomon Islands "to promote friendly relations with the natives." He was commander of the Australia Station, the Sydney-based Royal Navy squadron that protected Britain's interests in the southwest Pacific. (Transferred from the Royal Australian Navy Historical Collection)*

Following pages: *The new Australian National Maritime Museum building nears completion in Darling Harbour, Sydney. The work of leading Australian architect Philip Cox, AO, its dramatic design includes a 10-story hall to display full-rigged vessels, some of them suspended in midair.*

AO, to that other great Australian symbol of sails and waves, the Sydney Opera House.

The museum has been developed at a time when Australians, who have had a long but sometimes uneasy relationship with the sea, are reexamining their history and their myths. In 1988, Australians celebrated—and questioned—two hundred years of European settlement. The museum project began in 1985 as part of these bicentennial preparations.

It is a paradox that Australians, whose population is overwhelmingly concentrated in a few narrow coastal fringes and in port towns and cities, frequently seem fondest of their legends of the arid outback and the interior. The bicentennial celebrations reminded Australians that their origins were maritime and that many facts of their modern lives are still those of a nation entirely surrounded by the sea. The Australian National Maritime Museum, as well as taking a lead in preserving the nation's maritime heritage, uses its varied indoor and floating exhibitions to explain how this heritage has permeated so much of Australian history and culture.

Above: *Pearling lugger* John Louis, *far from its working grounds in Australia's tropical northwest, joins the ANMM vessel collection on Sydney Harbour. The 1957 auxiliary ketch came from a traditional working-sail fleet that was, until recently, a feature of the remote outback pearling town Broome.*

Opposite, left: *The world's fastest boat is in the museum's small craft collection. Australian engineer Ken Warby built* Spirit of Australia *and set the current world record at 511.11 kilometers per hour (317.5 miles per hour) in 1978. His plywood and fibreglass hydroplane is powered by a jet engine developing 22,000 newtons (5,000 pounds) of thrust.*

Top: *After a life's work guiding commercial shipping in waters as far apart as tropical Queensland and off stormy southern coastlines, this lightship now marks the entrance to the Australian National Maritime Museum's ship basin.*

Above: *Modern 18-foot skiff, its sails echoed by the Sydney Opera House, is of an ultra-fast class and is an all-Australian classic. The earliest in the collection, from 1917, was built of cedar and carried five times the crew and canvas. The 1987 flier is space age kevlar and carbon fibre, crewed by three trapeze artists.*

NOVA SCOTIA'S MARITIME MUSEUMS, HALIFAX AND LUNENBURG, NOVA SCOTIA

by David B. Flemming
Director, Maritime Museum of the Atlantic
and Heather-Anne Getson
Curator of Collections
Fisheries Museum of the Atlantic

Canada's Atlantic Provinces have long been the mainstay of the country's maritime economy. From the earliest European explorations during the 15th and 16th centuries to the development of the cod fishery on the off-shore banks of Newfoundland and Nova Scotia, Canada's access to the North Atlantic has led to the development of an important fishing, ship-building, and shipping industry for this region.

In the 1870s, Canada had the fourth largest merchant fleet in the world. Most of these vessels were registered in ports in Nova Scotia, New Brunswick, and Prince Edward Island, and "Bluenose" skippers and seafarers were renowned throughout the world. The importance of shipbuilding to the economies of these provinces and the involvement of their merchants and seafarers in the carrying trade and fisheries has provided a rich resource for maritime museums. This resource is even more important because the once proud and lucrative shipbuilding and shipping industries have declined dramatically throughout the 20th century.

Despite this decline, Nova Scotia and the other Atlantic Provinces continue to depend on the sea for much of their livelihood, through the exploitation of the rich North Atlantic fisheries. The salt fish production of the 19th and 20th centuries has given way to the fresh- and frozen-fish trade of the past seventy years. The development of a boatbuilding industry associated with inshore fishing has, until recently, been an important component of the maritime economy of Nova Scotia. Halifax, with the world's second largest natural harbour—Sydney, Australia, being the first—is a major North Atlantic port and boasts two con-

Opposite: *Perhaps the best-known Nova Scotian sailing vessel, the fishing schooner* Bluenose, *shown here in a race off Halifax in 1921, the year she was launched at Lunenburg. Besides being a successful fishing vessel, her speed enabled her to go undefeated in the five International Fishermen's Trophy series held between 1921 and 1938. She was lost off Haiti in January, 1946. A replica,* Bluenose II, *currently owned and operated by the Province of Nova Scotia, was launched in 1963, also from Lunenburg.*

Above: *Figureheads were important embellishments of sailing vessels, reflecting the pride of the ship owners in their vessels. This one is from a New Brunswick vessel that foundered in the Bay of Fundy in the 1840s.*

The Canadian Scientific Survey ship Acadia *was built in Newcastle-upon-Tyne in England in 1913. For 66 years she undertook hydrographic surveys along the east coast of Canada and into Hudson Bay. Acquired by the Fisheries Museum of the Atlantic in 1981, she provides visitors with an insightful look at hydrographic research, steamship technology, and life at sea in the Canadian Government Service during the first half of the 20th century. A high school oceanography program is conducted from her decks and from the museum's whaler. Ongoing restoration comprises a major part of the museum's operation.*

Above: *The William Robertson & Son Ship Chandlery. During the early years of this century, there were over a dozen ship chandleries located along Halifax's waterfront. William Robertson & Son operated on this site for over a hundred years before they closed in the mid-1970s. The museum has stocked this shop to what it would have looked like around the turn of the century, when it provided ship owners and seafarers with everything from "a needle to an anchor."*

Left: William D. Lawrence; *oil on canvas by an anonymous artist. This painting of the 2,459-ton* William D. Lawrence, *the largest wooden-hulled square-rigged sailing vessel ever built in Canada, is displayed at the home of her builder, William D. Lawrence, where another branch of the Nova Scotia Museum Complex is located at Maitland, Nova Scotia.*

tainer terminals and numerous bulk-loading facilities. Nova Scotia's seafaring heritage is preserved throughout the province at local museums with marine collections in communities like Yarmouth, Digby, Shelburne, Liverpool, Hantsport, Pictou, Parrsboro, Jeddore, Canso, and Louisbourg. The province of Nova Scotia, through the Nova Scotia Museum Complex, operates two large museums that reflect the seafaring past of Canada's Atlantic Provinces: the Maritime Museum of the Atlantic in Halifax and the Fisheries Museum of the Atlantic in Lunenburg.

THE MARITIME MUSEUM OF THE ATLANTIC

The Maritime Museum of the Atlantic in Halifax was founded in 1948 as a private museum to collect, research, and interpret the material history of the region's maritime heritage. In 1967, the collection became part of the provincial museum system, and after many temporary homes the museum was established in a permanent facility on the Halifax waterfront in 1981. Consisting of a 140-year-old ship chandlery complemented by a large modern exhibit wing, the museum houses over 17,000 artifacts. The exhibit galleries reflect various themes of marine history, except for the fishing industry, which is interpreted at the Fisheries Museum of the Atlantic.

The breadth and depth of the Maritime Museum of the Atlantic's collection is reflected in a visible storage area that forms part of the public galleries. Large collections of navigational instruments and equipment, naval ships' badges, and transoceanic cable equipment are but a few of the items displayed here.

Top: *A view of the original deckhouse of the coastal schooner* Rayo, *which was built at Economy, Nova Scotia in 1920. For 30 years, she traded between Canada's Maritime Provinces and New England.*

Above: *An interior view of a full-sized animated replica of the* Rayo's *deckhouse on display in the Days of Sail Gallery. The replica was built from lines taken off the original and furnished to the early 1940s, on the basis of interviews conducted with many of her former crew.*

The importance of the skills and crafts involved in seafaring are reflected in the ships' carpenters', riggers', and sailmakers' shops that form part of the Days of Sail gallery. Many of the tools used by 19th-century shipwrights, riggers, and sailmakers are displayed and demonstrated in their working context.

The museum's library is an important resource for researchers and includes a collection of over 15,000 photographs dating back to the 1860s. A large collection of nautical charts and a smaller assortment of vessel plans complement the photographic collection. An active research program, supported in part by volunteer research associates, provides information on a wide range of topics.

The region's rich shipbuilding heritage is captured in a collection of over one hundred marine paintings. Ship portraits provide important historical information about sailing vessels before the advent of the camera. One of the oldest such portraits in the museum collection is of the brig *James*, of Sydney, Nova Scotia, and built in Ship Harbour in 1826. Sailing vessels from Nova Scotia were involved in the carrying trade around the world during the 19th century.

Sir Samuel Cunard was born and raised in Nova Scotia and, before establishing the

Cunard Steamship line in England in 1840, had developed a thriving shipbuilding and shipping business in British North America. A special exhibit was mounted to commemorate his birth in Halifax in 1787. The Age of Steam gallery contains many excellent presentation models of Cunarders and other passenger and merchant steamships.

Ship models comprise another large and important part of the museum's collection. Besides being works of art, they serve an interpretive and educational function. A model of the bark *Calburga*, complete with figures of the crew, is used to explain the workings of a sailing ship. Built at Maitland, Nova Scotia, *Calburga* was the last Canadian bark in service and was lost off the coast of Wales in 1917.

The museum's interpretive programs offer a varied assortment of lectures, workshops, and demonstrations. Adults and children are given opportunities to build model ships, practice knot-tying skills, and sign on the museum's floating artifact, the Canadian Scientific Survey ship *Acadia*.

Throughout the summer, the *Acadia* is joined by various local and foreign vessels that make brief stays at the museum's wharves. Among the regular visitors is HMCS *Sackville*, the last of the World War II corvettes, which has been restored and is operated by the Canadian Naval Memorial Trust. Sail-training vessels and pleasure craft from around the North Atlantic are regular callers at the museum's wharves.

The museum has over forty small craft in its collection, and these are exhibited in either the Smallcraft Gallery or one of two boat sheds. Work boats of various types and methods of construction complement traditional pleasure craft used over the past one hundred years as well as a collection of canoes based on designs developed by Eastern Canada's native people prior to European contact. Included in the small-craft collection is the first of the popular Bluenose class sloops, launched in 1946, which were designed by William J. Roue, designer of the famous fishing-racing schooner *Bluenose* and the replica *Bluenose II*. Restoration of small craft is a major, ongoing commitment of the museum.

Its location on the Halifax waterfront makes the museum the focal point for many public events, and its wharves provide a safe haven for vessels ranging in size from small

Below: *Sail loft exhibit at the Fisheries Museum of the Atlantic. During the age of schooner fishing on the Banks, sail lofts were found in every fishing port.*

Right: *A demonstration of trawl setting at the Fisheries Museum of the Atlantic. On selected days during the summer, retired dory fishermen prepare to set trawl lines in Lunenburg's front harbour. They expertly chop their bait, attach it to fish hooks, and neatly coil the line in trawl tubs. Visitors watch as the gear is loaded in dories launched from the side of the museum schooner* Theresa E. Connor. *The trawl lines are set, and the men return to the schooner for a traditional "mug-up" of tea and talk to the visitors. Then out they go again to take in the day's catch.*

Following pages: *The Fisheries Museum of the Atlantic is located on the Lunenburg waterfront. The museum vessels include the schooner* Theresa E. Connor *and the steel side trawler* Cape Sable. *The museum buildings date to the turn of the 20th century and were originally part of W. C. Smith and Company, a fish processing firm.*

sailing sloops to large sail-training vessels. Modern merchant and naval vessels regularly pass by, providing a sharp contrast with the museum's collection and creating an important link with Nova Scotia's rich nautical past.

THE FISHERIES MUSEUM OF THE ATLANTIC

Lunenburg, located on Nova Scotia's south shore one hundred kilometers from Halifax, is well-known as a fishing port, and its tradition of marine-related skills dates back to the mid-1700s. During the age of sail, hundreds of Lunenburg schooners went to the fishing banks in search of cod.

That age has passed. Lunenburg is now home to a modern offshore fleet, with one of the largest fish-processing plants in North America. The spirit of the old town, however, has not changed. Intact areas of original streets abound, and each summer the days of schooner fishing are brought back to life on the waterfront at the Fisheries Museum of the Atlantic.

This museum had its start in 1967 as Lunenburg's Centennial of Confederation project. It began aboard the schooner *Theresa E. Connor*. This vessel was the last dory schooner to work from the port of Lunenburg, ending a twenty-five-year career in 1963. In 1966, the owners began negotiations to sell the vessel. With plans underway for the creation of a museum, members of the Lunenburg Marine Museum Society had the foresight to recognize the historic value of the schooner. They purchased the *Theresa E. Connor* and began a program to preserve this important symbol of Nova Scotia's maritime heritage. They also became a part of the Nova Scotia Museum Complex. The *Theresa E. Connor* has undergone several restoration projects. In 1988, a major portion of the vessel was restored forward of the break beam.

Thousands of artifacts, including a selection of small fishing craft and a steel side trawler, *Cape Sable,* have joined the *Theresa E. Connor*. Built in 1962 at the Boot-Leiden Shipyard, Leiden, Holland, the *Cape Sable* represents the type of motorized vessel that eventually replaced dory schooners like the *Theresa E. Connor*. The Fisheries Museum buildings were once part of a fish-processing firm and date back to the turn of this century. The museum has reduced its "Lunenburg" focus and specializes in the history of the fishing industry of Canada's Atlantic coast.

Although still in its infancy, the museum's Documentation Centre clearly reflects the institution's expanded focus. The library, archives, and photographic collection contain a wide variety of reference materials, and the museum theater features archival and modern documentaries concerning many aspects of the fisheries. The extensive exhibit program includes themes essential to the interpretation of the fishing industry. Donations and an ambitious acquisitions program assisted in developing a collection of approximately 20,000 items, ranging in size from herring scales to vessels, from everyday items to the unusual.

Activity is the key word at the Fisheries Museum. Demonstrations by retired fisher-

Opposite, top: *HMS* Asia *in Halifax Harbour, 1800; oil on canvas by Captain George Gustavus Lennock. Halifax has been an important naval station for over 200 years, first for the Royal Navy and later for the Royal Canadian Navy. Exhibits in the Navy Gallery reflect this long association. Captain Lennock painted this view of the naval dockyard while serving aboard HMS* Asia.

Opposite, bottom left: *The Hall of Inshore Fisheries contains a selection of Atlantic Canada's inshore fishing craft. Employment in the inshore fisheries has been a traditional way of life for fishermen all along the Atlantic coast. Various types of fishing boats have been developed to suit specific conditions in each area. Inshore fishermen follow a seasonal schedule in pursuit of lobster, mackerel, herring, and cod. Their domestic life is further explored in the Fisherman's Life Museum, a branch of the Nova Scotia Museum Complex, in Jeddore, Nova Scotia.*

Opposite, bottom right: *Sailor's Valentine brought back to Lunenburg in the 1920s by Captain Amplias Berringer. When salt fish were widely exported aboard schooners from Atlantic Canada, fishermen would often "make the trip down south" to the West Indies. Salt fish were replaced with cargoes of molasses, salt, sugar, and rum for the trip home. On these voyages, crewmembers often brought keepsakes home to loved ones.*

men and local inhabitants of fish filleting, small-craft construction, trawl setting, and other fisheries-related activities take place throughout the museum. Their various activities are not so much "role playing" or "animating" as reenactments of a familiar way of life. Visitors are encouraged to talk with the retired schooner fishermen as they prepare trawl for the *Theresa E. Connor.* A hands-on approach by visitors is promoted.

The specialized nature of the Fisheries Museum of the Atlantic makes it easily distinguishable from most other maritime museums. The institution's rapid growth attests to the dedicated support of the volunteer board of directors and of the Nova Scotia Museum and Fisheries Museum staff. The fishing industry has been an integral part of Canada's maritime heritage since the 16th century. The pursuit of fish led to some of the first European settlements in the Atlantic region. As a result, the Fisheries Museum of the Atlantic provides a link to the very roots of the Atlantic Provinces, documenting technological changes and preserving the vitality of past generations.

THE VANCOUVER MARITIME MUSEUM, VANCOUVER, BRITISH COLUMBIA

*by Robin Inglis, Director
and Leonard McCann, Curator*

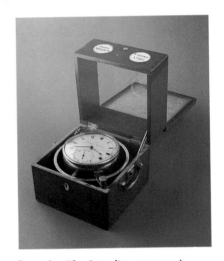

ancouver is located in the southern half of the northwest coast of North America, a region defined today by the U.S. states of Oregon, Washington, and Alaska and by the Canadian province of British Columbia. The Spanish, English, and American explorers and traders who visited the northwest coast at the end of the 18th century found it to be a land of high snow-capped mountains rising above densely forested fjords, inlets, and numerous islands, most often shrouded in the mists and fogs of its temperate climate. There was also the surprising discovery of rich and elaborate native societies, sustained by hunting and fishing, particularly of the abundant salmon. These societies displayed a high degree of technical skill and artistic achievement.

In the twenty years between the voyage of Juan Pérez, the Spanish colonial naval officer who sailed north from Mexico in 1774 to check on an imagined Russian challenge to Spanish power in the Americas, and the departure of the English navigator George Vancouver in 1794 after three summers of coastal survey, the northwest coast was firmly placed on the world map. When James Cook ran the coast in 1778, his contacts with the Indians precipitated a short-lived maritime fur trade. Just as importantly, his expedition refocused attention on the mystery of the Strait of Anian, a navigable waterway said to reach across the continent. The Spanish voyages and Vancouver's survey proved this to be illusory, but the Northwest Passage—sought from the Atlantic side since the 17th century and not conquered until the 1903-6 voyage of the Norwegian explorer Roald Amundsen—has always had a close association with the Vancouver Maritime Museum.

This association originates with the museum's founding in 1958 as part of the initiative to preserve the *St. Roch*, the two-masted auxillary schooner that served as a Royal Canadian Mounted Police arctic patrol ship for twenty-six years. Her great claim to fame was the first voyage through the passage from west to east, in 1940-42. She made the return voyage from Halifax to Vancouver in 1944 and, in 1950, again set out for Halifax, this time via the

Opposite: *The Canadian west coast's last remaining wood-hulled steam-engined tugboat, the* Master—*a regular presence in the Heritage Harbour, operated by one of the Vancouver Maritime Museum's affiliated societies. (Photo by W.D. McLaren)*

Above: *John Arnold's chronometer No. 176 used by George Vancouver during his survey of the northwest coast of America, 1792-94. (Photo by Henry Tabbers)*

Following pages: *Former armed services rescue craft* Black Duck, *maintained and operated as a work and program boat. (Photo by W.D. McLaren)*

Panama Canal. This trip made her the first ship to circumnavigate North America. Retired in Vancouver in 1954 and designated a National Historic Site in 1962, the *St. Roch* has been restored to her appearance during the 1944 voyage. She is the centerpiece of the museum and is operated by the Canadian Parks Service.

The museum's collections have grown gradually over the thirty years of its existence. They relate primarily to the early history of the coast and to the development of Vancouver as one of the continent's great ports. The museum has many fine ship models and an extensive collection of historic photographs that provide a record of maritime activity in the port from the late 19th century to today. A large number of the photographs are of ships that have had an ongoing relationship with Vancouver down the years.

Two of the oldest treasures in the collection are a rough "track chart" of the entire coast drawn in 1778 by William Bayly, the astronomer on Cook's third voyage, and Arnold 176, one of the chronometers carried by George Vancouver in 1792-94. The chart was donated, unappreciated, to the old Vancouver City Museum in the 1920s; the chronometer is the jewel in a small but representative collection of navigational instruments dating from the end of the 18th century.

By 1825, the maritime fur trade, based on the sea otter, had gone into dramatic decline. Overland trade from eastern Canada was gaining in importance and was dominated by the Hudson's Bay Company. The company brought the *Beaver*, the first engine-powered ship to operate along the coast, into service in 1836. An important section of the collection, including models, photographs, and memorabilia, highlights her fifty-six-year career as a fur trader, freighter, hydrographic surveyor, towboat and passenger vessel. The *Beaver* began the development of the province's coastal shipping services, which had become a vital lifeline and catalyst to economic activity by the end of the century.

Through paintings, models, and photographs, the collection traces the growth of what became the city of Vancouver from its start in a small sawmill on the water's edge amid the finest stand of timber on the coast. In 1864, the first overseas shipment of lumber went to Adelaide, Australia, beginning an export business that remains one of the industrial underpinnings of the province's economy as well as Canada's overseas links in the Pacific.

The arrival of the transcontinental railway in 1887 led directly to increased maritime activity. The collection reflects two obvious aspects of this: the coastal steamship services and the transpacific links. The B. C. Coast Service of the Canadian Pacific Railway, the Union Steamship Company, and the Canadian National Railway are represented by ship models, bells, fittings, uniforms, equipment, flags, chinaware, and other furnishings as well as by an extensive holding of archival material, historic photographs, and paintings. Dominating the collection related to overseas travel and trade is a builder's model of the *Empress of Asia,* representative of the "White Empresses" that were operated by the Canadian Pacific Railway and were among the finest transoceanic liners ever built. During the heyday of ocean travel in the 1920s and 1930s, a voyage to the Orient from Vancouver or a cruise around the world was an event to be cherished. The first *Empress of Japan*, which ran between Vancouver and

Above: *The Canadian-Australasian Line's* Aorangi II *leaving Vancouver for the last time under the Lion's Gate Bridge on May 14, 1953.*

Left: *Figurehead from the 19th-century sail-training brig H.M.S.* Pilot. *(Photo by Peter Fromm)*

Below: Beaver, *originally a Hudson's Bay Company supply vessel and the first steamship in the Pacific Northwest, 1836, shown in her last years as a towboat.*

Right: *Wreck of the C.P.R.'s coastal passenger vessel* Princess May *on Sentinel Island near Prince Rupert, British Columbia, August 5, 1910.*

Opposite, bottom: *Panoramic photograph of the Canadian Pacific Railway's new trans-Pacific base on the Vancouver waterfront in 1927.*

Japan between 1891 and 1922, had a special place in the hearts of the city's citizens. A fine model, paintings, photographs, fittings, and furnishings—including her bell, figurehead, and chronometer—illuminate her story and those of her successors.

Artifacts and archival materials also reflect a number of activities of a more local nature. The museum holds a significant collection of whale-processing tools, harpoons, and small whaling guns as well as important archival material related to the North Pacific whale fishery. Fishing in general is well represented by a selection of boat models, photographs, gear of all kinds, and canning equipment. Numerous items also deal with ship- and boat-building; there are shipwright and sailmaker's tools, casting patterns for ship fittings, half-hull models, as well as a small collection of locally built boats and small marine engines, both diesel and gasoline. A very important archival record, the papers of pioneer naval architect Gordon Hardie, provide an unusually comprehensive insight into early 20th-century shipbuilding and repair industries.

The activities of the port during the 20th century, while best represented in the collection of historic photographs, are also featured in displays of ship models from the age of sail to the modern period. Examples include the *Thermopolyae*, which made her name in the China tea and Australian wool trades before working out of Vancouver and other Canadian ports as a general cargo carrier; the *Silver Cypress* of the Java-Silver-Pacific line of the

Bottom left: *Sealing schooner* Thomas F. Bayard *off Vancouver Island in the early years of the 20th century. (Photo from Royal British Columbia Museum)*

Below left: *Barque S.F.* Tolmie *at Hastings Mill; oil painting by an anonymous artist, 1929. (Photo by Peter Fromm)*

Below right: Empress of Canada *near Yokohama with Mount Fuji in the background; oil painting by an anonymous artist, ca. 1920. (Photo by Peter Fromm)*

1930s; and the contemporary RoRo freighter *Skeena,* used to carry cars, trucks, and lumber on trailers. The museum also owns a series of tug models and has an extensive collection of fittings, equipment, engine components, builder's plates, and nameboards. Since the 1950s, Vancouver has grown to become an important center of the worldwide cruise ship industry. The major lines operate along the length of the North American west coast, with the June-October Alaska season out of Vancouver a particular highlight. The museum possesses a fine model of the P. and O. *Arcadia* and other items reflecting this important industry.

Because of Canada's longstanding British heritage, many interesting items have found their way into the collection, despite their having no obvious relevance to Canada's west coast. Among these are a letter from Admiral Nelson to Cuthbert Collingwood on the eve of the battle of Trafalgar; the figurehead of the Royal Navy's late 19th-century sail-training brig *Pilot;* and an exceptionally well executed model of an engine from a British destroyer of 1899.

The Vancouver Maritime Museum works closely with several affiliate groups, including the Underwater Archaeological Society of British Columbia, for which the museum holds an assortment of shipwreck artifacts, notably items from the wreck of the *Ericsson,* designed by John Ericsson, found off Vancouver Island in 1985; the S.S. *Master* Society, dedicated to the maintenance of the oldest surviving steam tug on the coast; the World Ship Society of Western Canada, which generously donated its collection of historic photograph negatives to the museum in 1986; and the Vancouver Wooden Boat Society, dedicated to the promotion and preservation of traditional skills and boats of particular historical interest. The most important ship in the museum's floating vessel collection is the *Thomas F. Bayard,* a Delaware Bay pilot cutter that, over its long history, served as an Alaska gold rush freighter, sealing schooner in the North Pacific, and lightship for fifty years at the mouth of the Fraser River. Built in New York in 1886, she is the oldest vessel in the Canadian Registry still afloat. Saved in 1978, and provided with a history through the museum's research efforts, the *Bayard* awaits restoration through the combined efforts of the museum and the *Thomas F. Bayard* Society.

The museum itself is looking toward a bright future. After a decade of substantial progress during the 1980s, the institution is ready to expand and move to a new location more closely identified with the activities of the port of Vancouver and the city's historic waterfront. More space will permit development of the collection through the acquisition of a great amount of material currently in private hands that, ideally, should come to the museum and further contribute to a unique record of the maritime heritage of Canada's west coast and her major port city—her window onto the Pacific, the ocean of the 21st century.

Above: *Painted window from the dining saloon of the* Empress of Japan, *built in 1890. (Photo by Henry Tabbers)*

Opposite, top left: *Operational model of the portside engine of an 1899 destroyer made in 1966 by Ian Main of Vancouver.*

Opposite, top right: *Rough track chart of the northwest coast of America prepared in 1778 by William Bayly, astronomer on James Cook's third voyage to the Pacific, showing the progress of Cook's* Resolution *and* Endeavor. *(Photo by Peter Fromm)*

Opposite, bottom: Empress of Japan *in Vancouver in the 1890s. The figurehead is in the collection of the museum.*

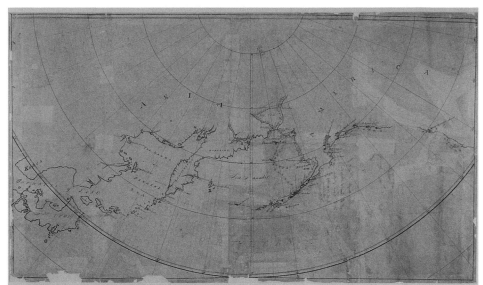

THE VIKING SHIP MUSEUM, ROSKILDE

by Jan Skamby Madsen, Museum Director

Opposite: *Replica of a 14-meter merchant vessel from Roskilde Fjord. Since Viking boatbuilders did not use saws, all timber was cleaved with wedges and dressed with axe and adze. Trunks from eleven large oak trees were needed for the construction of this ship. (Photo by Lotzbeck)*

Above: *The Viking Ship Museum seen from the fjord.*

During the quarter of a millennium from 800 to 1050 A.D., the peoples of Scandinavia marked the course of European history more than they have at any time since. Tens of thousands of Swedes, Norwegians, and Danes left their native soil for the uncertain promise of a difficult existence at sea and abroad. Some of them were peaceful traders, carrying merchandise in their ships, or farmers in search of unploughed land. But others were envoys of war, striving, sword in hand, for power and riches. This is the period of Scandinavian history known as the Viking Age.

The Vikings sailed halfway around the world in their open boats and vastly extended its known boundaries. They traveled farther to the north and west than any European had ever done before, founding new and lasting colonies in the Faroe Islands and Iceland and building settlements in Greenland and even on the North American continent (L'Ance aux Meadows, Newfoundland), 500 years before Columbus. They penetrated Russia along rivers and opened a trade route to Asia.

What was the background for the grand ships and seamanship of the Vikings? This is one of the major questions the Viking Ship Museum is designed to answer.

The Viking Ship Museum is a specialized institution concerned with the study of Scandinavian ship- and boatbuilding culture, especially in prehistoric times and the Middle Ages; that is, up to around 1500 A.D. The museum's work includes excavating, recording, research, conservation, and exhibition, as well as the publication of archaeological, historical, ethnographic, and other materials. The Viking Ship Museum and the Institute of Maritime Archaeology of the Danish National Museum cooperate closely on most activities, both in terms of research and excavation and in terms of conservation and publications.

This all began in 1962 when the National Museum undertook the excavation of five Viking ships. These ships had been deliberately filled with stones and sunk in Roskilde Fjord sometime between A.D. 1000 and 1050, in order to block entrance to Roskilde by enemy ships. Roskilde had become the largest town on Zealand (Sjaelland) by the end of the Viking

In 1962, a cofferdam was built around the excavation in Roskilde Fjord where the Viking ships were sunk, and the area was pumped free of water.

Age, the first half of the 11th century. King Harald Blåtand (Harold Bluetooth) had built his manor and a church there, making Roskilde his main residence. The town lies at the inner end of a shallow fjord forty-five kilometers from the open sea. The water level was so low in many places that special channels (fairways) had to be negotiated in order to reach Roskilde from the sea. It was one of these channels that was blocked by sinking the Viking ships.

The vessels represent a wide variety of types, all dating from about 1000 A.D. They include a longship of thirty meters length, two merchant ships, a smaller man-of-war, and a fishing boat—all types not previously documented by archaeological finds. Viking ships had been found in Norway, where kings and chieftains were buried with their ships in grave mounds at Gokstad and Oseberg. These ships were yachts, however, carefully executed for

Below: *A view of the exhibition hall of the Viking Ship Museum with display of a merchant vessel.*

Opposite: *Diver exploring a shipwreck from the Middle Ages.*

Following pages: *Viking ship replicas under sail in Roskilde Fjord with the towers of Roskilde Cathedral in the background.*

royalty. They tell us little about everyday conditions for the Viking sailor on his long voyages as merchant or warrior. The ships from Roskilde were obviously vessels chosen for use in the blockade because they were old and worn by years of hard use.

The salvage work in 1962 was carried out within a cofferdam, and the ships were excavated during the three summer months by a hardworking group of students directed by Dr. Olaf Olsen and Dr. Ole Crumlin-Pedersen. After the excavation, the wood was recorded in full-scale tracings giving all details of each plank.

Even before the excavation was completed in 1962, consideration had been given to the question of a future home for the ships. They needed a roomy, permanent place where they could be both restored and exhibited. The best site was found in the old town of

Roskilde, from which the ships had undoubtedly sailed in the first place to create the blockade. The museum was offered a place on the waterfront, facing the natural habor, where ships rode at anchor a thousand years ago.

As soon as a sufficient number of pieces had passed through the preservation treatment, restoration and reconstruction of the first ship began. By this time, in 1968, the museum building had been completed, and it was soon turned into a living workshop, centering on the ancient ships. This workshop-museum was officially opened in June 1969. The public has been able to watch the assembly of the five ships as well as follow the actual excavation on film.

A long series of studies has been undertaken in the field since the five Viking ships were lifted from the bottom of Roskilde Fjord. As often as possible, some part of the museum's laboratory activity takes place in the exhibition area, so that visitors can watch the work of recording and preparing newly found timbers and other artifacts for conservation.

Below: *Viking ship replicas under sail.*

Opposite: *Drawing of the five Viking ships from Roskilde Fjord.*

This situation offers an optimal relationship with the public. When a site is excavated, visitors are invited to see the fieldwork. The museum's exhibitions are designed to take advantage of this close connection among the public, the finds, and the museum staff.

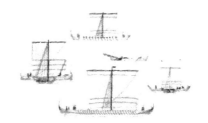

The museum also conducts a special series of boatbuilding projects meant to show the use of various materials for the construction of so-called primitive boats. In 1980, a skin-boat was built as part of this series. This "umiaq" was made by seven elders from the Nanortalik in southwest Greenland. In April 1981, William Commanda, a former chief of the River Desert Algonquin Band near Maniwaki, Quebec, visited Roskilde with his wife, Mary. They demonstrated the art of building a traditional Algonquin birch-bark hunting canoe. In April, May, and June 1985, the seventy-three-year-old Nootka Indian George Louie, from Vancouver, visited the museum with his two sons and built a traditional whale-hunting canoe of a single fifteen-meter-long red-cedar log. In May 1986, Kovan Kavang, a member of the Punan Bah people of Borneo, demonstrated the building of a traditional dugout with sewn planks on

both sides. In April 1990, Aymara Indians from Lake Titicaca in Bolivia showed how to build a reed boat; this work was carried out by the famous boatbuilder Paulino Esteban and two of his sons.

These boatbuilding projects offer an opportunity to make exact and scholarly records of the building processes while also giving the public unique demonstrations.

The museum's activities are not restricted to within the walls of the building. The museum's setting makes it ideal for the presentation of ancient boat types in their own element—water—which lies just outside the museum windows. A small fleet of boats of traditional Scandinavian design has been gathered, boats with Viking-ship characteristics. These include, for example, an eleven-meter Norwegian Nordland fishing boat with a square rig, and an eighteen-meter "church boat," meant to be rowed by twenty people.

These and other similar boats are kept in working order and are occasionally sailed, both to keep alive the skill of handling them and to provide a practical background to the

Below, and opposite left and top right: *Working on the merchant vessel replica.*

Opposite, bottom right: *Test sailing the merchant vessel replica.*

work of restoring and interpreting Viking ships.

The museum's collection of sailing boats in working order is kept in the Roskilde Boatyard, from where they also sail. From 1982 to 1984, visitors there could follow the building of an exact, full-scale copy of the small Viking trading ship seen in the museum. The copy was launched in October 1984 and has been used in recent years for experimental trips in order to test its sailing qualities in various wind and weather conditions. The museum staff was able to demonstrate the entire building process. The construction made clear how difficult it is for modern boatbuilders to achieve the level of craftsmanship shown by the Vikings.

THE MUSÉE DU BATEAU, DOUARNENEZ

by Denis-Michel Boell, Conservateur

One of the most intriguing and moving exhibits for visitors to the Musée du Bateau is a piece of a wreck, about five meters long. The massive keel section holds a dozen pieces of the ship's framework on which some planking remains. Along the keel the mast seating can be seen and here and there remains of keel bolts. This skeleton, discovered in a peat bog near Douarnenez Bay, is all that remains of the thousands of sardine luggers that fished under sail at the beginning of the century around Brittany.

The Breton shores still offer up the fascinating spectacle of wooden hulls peeping out of the sand or mudflats in certain areas. These are the last remnants of the fleets of working vessels that gave this seafaring region, perched on the westernmost point of the European continent, part of its prosperity.

It was in these boat graveyards, a little over ten years ago, that a few enthusiasts decided to examine, note, and collect this precious technical evidence of Brittany's seafaring past. Some of these men, who saved part of France's maritime history by examining the last evidence of the age of working sail, are the founders of the recently created Musée du Bateau. Grouped around the Treizour association are instructors from the Regional Federation for Maritime Culture and the staff of the maritime historical and ethnological magazine *Le Chasse-Marée*. In 1985, after four years of operation as a fleet museum centered on the local maritime identity, this team founded a museum designed to display to their best advantage an excellent collection of small- and medium-sized craft brought together over several years. They were fully supported by the town council of Douarnenez, a fishing port of some 17,000 inhabitants.

The collection is unique in France because of its diversity and the number of exhibits—nearly 200. The great majority of these are working boats, generally from six to ten meters long, used in days gone by for inshore and river fishing, short-range cargo carrying, ferrying across rivers and inlets, or as bumboats—small craft used to peddle provisions and

Opposite: *The sardine lugger* Telenn Mor, *built in 1983, a replica of a local working sailing boat from the turn of the century, used by the museum for school groups. (Photo by D.M. Boell)*

Following pages: Amitié, *one of six "Bantry boats," a copy of the Bantry longboat of the 17th-century frigate* Résolue. *The boat is being sailed by "the friends of the museum" who train every weekend for the Atlantic Challenge rowing race. (Photo by D.M. Boell)*

small wares to ships anchored offshore. Few of them were destined for more glamorous tasks. On the contrary, most have been chosen to bear witness to the everyday life of French seafolk and riverfolk. The criterion for selection was their degree of representation of a specific craft or of a local tradition.

Juxtaposing them reveals the extreme diversity of shape, fitting out, and rigging, the variety of their uses, and the traditions of the coastal and river communities in which they were the tools of trade. From Flanders to the Basque country, all the Channel and Atlantic coastlines are richly represented: the Mediterranean coast from Catalonia to the area of Nice is less strongly represented because the quest for exhibits in this region was started later. Brittany is, of course, particularly well covered, and some of the most characteristic craft, such as the Carantec cutter from the north coast or the lugger from the south coast, exist in several versions, varying according to different shipyards, ages, and uses. On the other hand, several items are representative of types of craft that were formerly in widespread use in their areas of origin but which have now become very rare, sometimes unique. One such case is the *Saint-Lazare*, a "mourre de pouar" from the Gulf of Lions, with its characteristic

Below: *The Musée du Bateau first started in 19th-century industrial buildings on the riverside at Port-Rhu. It then spread to Place de l'Enfer into wooden sheds which it uses for building and restoration. (Photo by B. Ficatier)*

Left: *Breton lobster sloop, Portuguese "moliceiro," Norwegian "oselvar," Mediterranean "mourre de pouar," and clinker-built hulls from Channel beaches are put together in the central hall of the museum. Visitors have an opportunity to compare the various ways in which vessels are built and rigged, painted and decorated, and to appreciate the various shapes of their hulls. (Photo by M. Thersiquel)*

Below left: *Displayed full size, the boats are not only to be seen but also to be touched. (Photo by M. Thersiquel)*

Below: *The boat storage areas are also open to the public so that visitors can have a look at the full collection. (Photo by J.M. Chauvet d'Arcizas)*

shape and lateen sail, which is now the last surviving example of its type. The Normandy "caïque" and the Gironde "filadière" are known to exist only in one other example elsewhere. Such a collection could not be assembled today because during the last ten years many of these last representatives of centuries-old local traditions have disappeared. One-tenth of the collection comes from other parts of Europe: a "dorna" from Spain, a "moliceiro" and a "bateira" from Portugal, yoles and clinker-built boats from England, the Shetlands, the Faroes, and even from Norway. These varied origins permit visitors to compare and contrast technological traditions, nautical characteristics, and different customs in the fitting out and decoration of boats, which distinguish coastal communities from one another; it is also possible to note other aspects that the boats have in common.

This collection is not exclusively maritime, since one quarter of the boat exhibits come from inland waters: a Loire "futreau," a Tarn flat-bottomed boat, an Adour "chaland," a Lake Geneva "barque," a Grand-Lieu Lake sailing punt, a sailing punt from the Brière Marshes, and even a Severn River coracle.

About forty of the boats are leisure craft, which demonstrate the history of pleasure sailing in the 20th century. Besides local models inspired by working boats, there are examples of several famous series of monotypes, keeled and dagger-board dinghies, modest sporting boats, folding canvas kayaks and canoes from the time of the first "holidays with pay," paddle-propelled skiffs, and rowing yoles. Some of the most exceptional items in the collection are on display in this section: the minute paddle-propelled skiff on which an officer paddled down most of the major European rivers in 1880, a Thames dinghy imported around 1895 by a frequent visitor to the island of Bréhat as a gift for his Scottish fiancée, and the last clinker-built dagger-board dinghy from Le Havre, saved from destruction at the beginning of the last war by its young builder and preserved by him for the rest of his life.

Efforts are being made to enlarge this collection, with the search for missing regional craft, a collection program for larger craft, and reconstructions of the many kinds of sailing boats that have disappeared but about which sufficient information can still be gathered. Such replicas as the sardine lugger *Telenn Mor* or the "sinago" *Souvenir*, launched in 1987, already sail alongside older boats, such as the upper Normandy pilot riverboat *Ariane*, launched in 1927.

The primary attraction of the Musée du Bateau is that it displays almost exclusively life-size craft and only rarely has recourse to scale models. An old cannery, converted to house the exhibits, skillfully restored by an architect who respected the past of the building, offers enough space to display most craft under ten meters in length with sails spread. The visitor is at first surprised by the explosion of colors, sails dyed brown, ocher, blue, or red, varnished or painted hulls, sometimes richly decorated, as is the case of the Portuguese craft.

Visitors wander freely from area to area among boats that they can touch and look at from every angle, from hull bottom to masthead, thanks to multi-level access, ramps, and catwalks.

Left: *The Douarnenez '88 Sail Festival involved 850 traditional craft and 3,000 crewmen. (Photo by J.M. Chauvet d'Arcizas)*

The exhibition's first purpose is the juxtaposition of various craft illustrating the main families of boatbuilding: clinker-built hulls or smooth-hulled boats made of hide or canvas, types of rigging, and different shapes of sails. To complement this, other exhibitions offer a more sociological approach: the crafts' different uses, life aboard, decoration. These instructional exhibits are completed by tableaux using wax figures around real boats. Here can be seen three sardine fishermen having their meal on board an open lugger, sheltering under their sail spread as a tent over the lowered mast; there are two shipwrights planking a small boat in a reconstructed boatyard; farther on, a small crab boat can be seen being winched up the slipway of a tiny, simple harbor. These tableaux put the boats back into their settings. By adding to the number of these "ecological units," the museum has set out to depict a panorama of the nautical activities of coastal and waterway cultures.

From the time of its founding, the museum has been intended not only as a place of learning for the general public, but also as a crossroads for the exchange of knowledge and knowhow about boats, boatbuilding, and sailing. The training center Les Ateliers de l'Enfer ("Hell's Workshops"), installed on the ground floor of the building, hosts about twenty apprentices every year who, in small teams, build three or four craft of greatly varying types. These are replicas of museum exhibits, reconstructions from plans, or results of verbal inquiries. This activity enhances the museum's appearance, offering the visitor concrete examples of the written explanations of the exhibits. Spread out around the museum and the sheds on Place de l'Enfer ("Hell's Square"), boatbuilding is an open-air permanent attraction in surroundings enlivened by the buzz of saws and the thud of mallets, the fire under the steam caldron and the forge, the air redolent with the sharp smells of pitch and freshly sawn wood.

Each launching is an opportunity for a local celebration that attracts enthusiasts from afar. In 1986 and 1988, the people of Douarnenez held great meetings of traditional sailing boats and ships. Thousands of enthusiasts and spectators came together to share the extraordinary sight of 850 old vessels of all sizes and origins sailing together in this bay, which is open to the western winds and is one of the most beautiful natural nautical amphitheaters in western Europe. The third show, in 1992, will coincide with the inauguration of the museum harbor, a decisive step in the development of the Musée du Bateau. This project sets out to create in the heart of the town a space for permanent shows, exhibits, and events based on the area's seafaring heritage.

On this new stretch of water, created by transforming the tidal rivermouth into a deepwater port, the museum will find its true nautical dimension. Originally founded to house the last evidence of a civilization based on working sail, the Musée du Bateau, thanks to the floating museum, will become a decisive factor in the renewal of the old seafaring heart of Douarnenez, but more than that—it will be highly instrumental in the rebirth in France of a genuine maritime culture.

Opposite, top: *View of the '88 Sail Festival. (Photo by J.M. Chauvet d'Arcizas)*

Opposite, bottom right: *Jean-Pierre Philippe, boatbuilder, shipwright, and one of the founders of the museum, building his sixth boat—the 11-meter lobster sailing vessel* An Askell. *(Photo by B. Ficatier)*

Opposite, bottom left: *Launching the lobster sailing vessel* An Askell *in September, 1989. The launching provided an opportunity for popular entertainment. (Photo by M. Thersiquel)*

FRANCE
MUSÉE DE LA MARINE,

PARIS

by François Bellec, Directeur

One day during 1748, Louis-Henri Duhamel du Monceau, general inspector of France's navy, asked King Louis XV for his personal collection of ship and shipyard-machinery models. Duhamel du Monceau had long dreamed of creating a school in Paris for naval architects and shipbuilders in order to bring together and solidify the basics of shipbuilding.

Count de Maurepas, minister of the navy, gave Duhamel du Monceau full charge of the collection, which was deposited in the Louvre. Thus, Duhamel du Monceau became the first curator of a national maritime museum. Thanks to his efforts, the Musée de la Marine shares with the Soviet Fleet Museum of Leningrad, created by Peter the Great, the honor of being the world's oldest maritime museum.

Since the naval collections in the Louvre were housed near the Royal Library and the Academy of Science, they were abruptly closed half a century later by revolutionaries. On August 7, 1793, the National Convention, with Georges Jacques Danton presiding, coolly declared that academies and literary societies were obviously of no national interest and were therefore to be closed.

Although the revolutionaries looked unkindly on the maritime museum, the Revolution itself ultimately provided the museum with many contributions. The collections of models of many noble émigrés, as well as the royal collection, were confiscated, but many of the most significant pieces were recovered, including the magnificent models belonging to the duke of Orléans, himself a victim of the guillotine.

After a long period of political disturbance, the museum was reorganized and reopened to become a popular maritime museum. This occurred when France was enthusiastic over a maritime revival following the humiliating period of the Napoleonic wars. All of France then followed with national passion the overseas achievements of the nation's explorers. The museum's collections were greatly enhanced by the addition of wonderful ship models, paintings, and sculptures from naval bases, art museums, and such national palaces as Versailles and Trianon.

Opposite: *Grouping of exotic boat models of fishing vessels and merchant and military ships from the 16th to the 19th centuries.*

Above: *The landscape and fountains surrounding the Palais de Chaillot in which the collections of the Musée de la Marine are housed.*

Following pages: The Cherbourg Roads, *oil on canvas, 1822, by Louis-Philippe Crépin (1772-1851). The semaphore post was installed on l'île Pelée near Cherbourg in 1806.*

This was still a difficult period for French museums. The Musée Dauphin, named in honor of the duke of Angoulême, great admiral of France, was set up by order of Charles X on December 27, 1827. Three years later, the first visitors crowded the rooms. They had not come to admire the collection, however, and expressed interest only in getting their hands on swords, pistols, and axes for the purpose of a new insurrection: the July Revolution.

Gathered during a century troubled by revolutions and wars, the Musée de la Marine's collections have been jeopardized by various other dangers, including the occasional loan. For instance, through King Louis Philippe, several models were loaned to the official court painter Théodore Gudin. In spite of repeated requests over a period of many years, Gudin failed to return the models, and in fact they made their way back to the museum only after the famous artist's death. The models were in a state of destruction, having been dealt blows from swords and blasts of shot so they would give a more realistic effect when used as models for painting naval engagements.

The collection had to face yet other dramatic events. One of the museum's greatest curators, Morel-Fatio, an official painter for the navy, gave the collection a new touch of fine art. He died suddenly on March 1, 1871, while watching from the roof of the museum German soldiers march into Paris: a grim moment of the Franco-Prussian War. A few days later, *communards*—members of the commune of Paris—set fire to the Tuileries palace, and the flames very nearly reached the Louvre and the maritime museum.

Since 1943, the Musée de la Marine has been housed in the Palais de Chaillot, which overlooks one of the most beautiful angles of Paris, facing the Eiffel Tower and the Champ de Mars. During the 16th century, this was the site of the country residence of Marie de Médicis. The Palais de Chaillot was erected in 1937 on the occasion of a universal exhibition. The Musée de la Marine shares one of the wings of this wide building with the Museum of Mankind; the building is home to one other museum and to a theater.

Thanks to the wealth of its collection, the Musée de la Marine represents the French maritime tradition and the special connections between the French people and the ocean. The activities of the Musée de la Marine are further amplified by the museum's connections with other institutions. In fact, the museum's Parisian staff is responsible for fourteen maritime museums set up along the seaside, on both the Atlantic and Mediterranean coasts. This allows the museum to make a wonderful contribution to France's maritime heritage, but it is also a difficult task. The museum's collections are vast enough to permit it to operate several other important exhibitions, most of them housed in magnificent old historic buildings. The largest are in the vicinity of the main naval bases, in Brest, Port-Louis, Rochefort, and Toulon. For instance, a maritime museum is located in the castle of Brest, which was built from the 13th to the 17th centuries on Roman foundations from the 2nd century. In Port-Louis, the museum is housed in a 17th-century citadel, and in Rochefort it is in the Hôtel de Cheusses, the 17th-century residence of France's fleet admirals.

The most spectacular models on display in the museums of Paris and Toulon are six

Opposite, top: *Trial model built by Jouffroy d'Abbans in 1783. A steamship invented by Jouffroy d'Abbans sailed successfully on the Saone and the Rhône rivers in 1782. The purpose of this model was to convince the Parisian Academies of the reality of that accomplishment.*

Opposite, bottom left: *Figurehead from the prow of the corvette* La Triomphante, *1830–79.*

Opposite, bottom right: *A large, late 18th-century scale model of the 120-gun* L'Océan *greets visitors to the museum.*

Following pages: The Harbour of La Ciotat, *by Jean-Baptiste de la Rose, 1664, a member of a famous family of maritime artists.*

large-scale ship models built in the 17th and 18th centuries for instruction purposes. These beautiful works are major sources of knowledge of French naval history.

The impressive golden ornaments from *La Réale,* the galleys' admiral's flagship, offer a sense of actual proportion to an outstanding collection of galley models. Glorifying the Sun King, Louis XIV, this exceptional carved wooden construction is a powerful evocation of the sumptuous royal fleet.

A famous series of paintings of French harbours by Claude-Joseph Vernet recounts the life of the harbours and dockyards in the last quiet years before the French Revolution. At that same period, Queen Marie Antoinette's fully ornamented longboat sailed on Versaille's Grand Canal in the company of the court's impressive leisure flotilla. The carved bow and stern of the queen's boat are among the museum's treasures.

During the 18th century, the French navy fought and won major battles in the Indian Ocean and the West Indies. Its success helped the young United States of America gain independence, and French Admiral Count de Grasse helped make possible the victory at Yorktown.

Relics of Jean François de Galaup, the comte de Lapérouse's expedition were recovered in the lagoon of Vanikoro, the ever-cloudy and thus somehow baleful island of the Solomons. They suggest the misery and courage of the French explorers who covered the world: Bougainville, Lapérouse, d'Entrecasteaux, Dumont d'Urville, and many others. Other relics recall the wide-ranging expeditions England and France carried out in the Pacific

Left: *Napoléon's barge, 1811. This longboat was built in three weeks in Antwerp. The sculptures are by Collet.*

Ocean in the name of civilization and science. Scientists, instrument makers, and clockmakers gave navigators the most precious gift of the age of discoveries: longitude.

The period of the Napoléonic wars are recalled in the Paris collection by a fascinating longboat built for the emperor's visit to Antwerp. To get this oversized barge into the museum, a hole had to be opened in one of the building's walls.

More touching, perhaps, is a ship model of the frigate *Muiron,* which was kept in Napoléon's private apartment in Malmaison. Also moving is the tiny ivory model given the empress Marie Louise on the occasion of the birth of her son, Napoléon II, known as the king of Rome.

The Musée de la Marine is grateful to Admiral Paris, one of its great curators, for an outstanding collection of exotic models. These were built based on notes he made during three journeys around the world—the first under the command of Dumont d'Urville—in the middle of the 19th century. Today, they are the only records of many long-gone traditions of overseas shipbuilding.

Admiral Paris was one of the pioneers of steamships, and the Musée de la Marine owns reminders of the French engineers who contributed to that great scientific and technological venture: Jouffroy d'Abbans, Sauvage, Normand, and particularly Dupuy de Lome, who conceived the *Napoléon* in 1850 and *La Gloire* launched nine years later, the first armored cruiser in the world, the archetype of the modern fleets.

The museum's two libraries, including one in Rochefort specializing in maritime surgery and chemistry, hold roughly 50,000 books and manuscripts, among which is a large heritage from the 18th century. There are also 350,000 documents, shipyard drawings, and photographs that make the Musée de la Marine a center for studies and research on French naval history and shipbuilding.

The collection in the Palais de Chaillot is a museum of maritime adventure over the ages and from the points of view of many nations. Temporary exhibits present charts and manuscripts from the fascinating collections of the Bibliothèque Nationale or the Archives de France.

With its young staff, the museum also remains in close contact with this century. Sea captains, historians, archaeologists, and journalists often visit the museum, among them such well-known figures as Jacques-Yves Cousteau and the famous skippers engaged in the yacht races that have given France a new maritime heritage. The museum is planning a new museum that will be the first naval collection devoted to yachting and nautical sports, with holdings that will range from artifacts of early yacht clubs to the most modern technology used in transoceanic contests or the America's Cup.

France lost much of her maritime heritage through wars and, it must be said, through negligence. The Musée de la Marine has assumed a major responsibility for preserving what remains. Working closely with other museums, it is engaged in the ongoing and exciting discovery of the long French maritime tradition.

Top: *The majestic golden ornaments of the galley* La Réale *by Le Brun, 1674. Many events, such as concerts, lectures, and social events take place under this glorious homage to Louis XVI. Commandant Jacques-Yves Cousteau received his crystal sword of Academician here.*

Above: *The bow of the 18th-century model of* La Réale.

Following pages: *This rare, late 18th-century painting of* La Réale *by an anonymous painter was purchased by the museum recently.*

FRANCE
THE MUSÉE DE LA PÊCHE, CONCARNEAU

by Hervé Gloux, Conservateur

ocated at the westernmost point of the European continent, Brittany became part of France only in the 15th century. Its population, Celtic in origin, has always been involved with the sea, and since earliest times fishing of all kinds has been practiced here. On the southern coast of the Brittany peninsula, the city of Concarneau was built on a small rocky island well inside a protected bay. Surrounding this active fishing port are granite ramparts over a thousand years old. In 1961, a collection of models of fishing boats was exhibited in an old army barracks, which later became a Maritime Training Institute. Concarneau is also a popular summer resort, welcoming tourists from all over Europe. This, too, was an important factor in deciding to establish a museum here. No site was more appropriate for a maritime museum, and collections were rapidly organized to present the history of different fishing techniques practiced all over the world.

In 1990, the museum achieved an important goal and took what might be called its definitive form when it occupied a building of over 200 square meters built to the museum's needs and specifications. On entering, the visitor sees facsimilies of arrows, harpoons, and fishing hooks, arranged to present the chronological evolution of fishing from prehistoric times to the development of mechanically propelled boats. To present the exhibits as clearly as possible, the staff decided on exhibits in the form of dioramas. A diorama is essentially a panorama, usually on a small scale, constructed with the aid of a model or models within the framework of a painted background. The principle behind a "madrague," or stationary net, for example, can be demonstrated more effectively using a model than a long descriptive text.

Following the history of fishing, the industries related to fishing are represented by models of wooden boats, their sails, and equipment. There follow models of mechanically propelled vessels in three categories: steam, gasoline, and diesel, as well as exhibits of canning techniques and facilities and navigational instruments. There is also an extensive

Opposite: *The only land access to the Ville Close, or Enclosed City, is this ancient drawbridge. The Musée de la Pêche is situated within the ramparts of this fortified, rocky island in the middle of the harbor of Concarneau which was called Conq or Kung by the Picts who inhabited it in A.D. 692.*

Above: *Diorama of a fishing trawler at night.*

Following pages: *Concarneau is the third most important fishing port in France—but the first, if one considers the arrival of the tropical tuna. This bird's-eye view of the town, a center of tourism and pleasure craft, shows the harbor surrounding the Ville Close.*

aquarium to acquaint the visitor with all the varieties of fish and crustacean found on the Brittany coast.

Coastal fishing led to the development of various types of boat depending on the waters in which they fished and the nature of the catch. By the use of models and dioramas, visitors can distinguish among the "bisquine" of Cancale (a type of fishing smack from the small Breton port of Cancale), the "chaloupe" or long boat used for sardine fishing, the lobster boat, and the "pinasse," a flat-bottomed craft used in the shallow waters of the Bordeaux region. Whaling, so important in the past, is represented by that most beautiful example of naval architecture, the "baleinière des Açores," or the whaling ship of the Azores. At this point, a tour of the museum can be interrupted by a visit to the museum wharf located directly in the center of the fishing port itself. Here one can see an actual fishing boat over thirty-five meters in length that has been out of active service since 1982—an opportunity to get a firsthand feeling for the life of a fisherman.

The museum tour continues with boats used for the cod fishing off the banks of Newfoundland and Iceland that brought so much wealth and glory to Brittany. Yet perhaps the most spectacular exhibits are the *Hémérica*, the museum's own trawler, shown as it would be in operation, floating in a 2,000-liter basin, and the model of a longitudinal section

Below: *Model of a North American fishing schooner used extensively in cod fishing. Known all over the world for their superior performance, these vessels are distinguished by their yachtlike appearance and speed.*

Above: *Concarneau around the end of the 19th century, at the apogee of the sardine fishing industry.*

Left: *The elegant and racy lines of this whaler from the Azores contrast with those of Russian and Japanese whaling boats. While still perfectly useful in a traditional way, it appears to have more of a kinship to sport fishing craft than to industrial fishing vessels.*

Left: *In the Galerie Vitrée, or Glazed Gallery, a reconstructed section of a wooden boat showing the details of its construction.*

Following pages: *Eleven years of negotiations were needed to create the opportunity to visit fishing boats within the framework of a museum. Moored to the 70-meter jetty is the 35-meter Hémérica (rear), a traditional trawler built in Saint Nazaire in 1957 and opened to the public as part of the Musée de la Pêche in 1987, Le Racleur d'Ocean, or Sea Scraper (center), a 17-meter tuna fishing boat, and a modern fiberglass coastal fishing boat (foreground) that is used as a service craft by the museum.*

of the last semi-industrial "concarnois," the typical fishing vessel of Concarneau, minutely detailed and illuminated. Concarneau itself owes its position as the third fishing port of France to the use of trawling nets in the form of cones or funnels (a type of net known as a *chalut*, thus the name *chalutier*, or trawler). No wonder the museum dwells in loving detail on this type of fishing boat.

Another activity that has brought recognition to this port is tuna fishing. The visitor can examine the first tuna-fishing sailboats. To emphasize the elegance of these vessels, the museum studio made a one-sixth scale model with masts and sails but without one side of the hull so as to allow an appreciation of the intricacy of the construction. Visitors can also see models from the era of clipper ships, a type that has, of course, disappeared from the Brittany coast to be replaced by the net-seining tuna-fishing boats with their elaborate freezing equipment.

The wealth of Brittany's maritime heritage merits in-depth study, and with the astonishing diversity of fishing methods, all of which are continually evolving, the museum finds itself going beyond its traditional goal of studying the past to look more toward the future, a

Left: *Panorama of the room exhibiting the coastal fisheries with a mizzenmaster traditional on the southern coasts of Brittany (foreground) and a single-masted cutter typical of the northern peninsula (background).*

Opposite: *Diorama showing the maritime activities of the French coast during the 18th century, constructed according to the research of Duhamel du Monceau, Inspecteur General de la Marine of the Academie des Sciences, whose work was published in 1777. If certain concepts have endured the passage of time, others, such as the "dreige," have disappeared. This technique consisted of allowing the sails to drop into the water while the current dragged the boat and its nets.*

future that is increasingly international. Within this broader scope, the visitor can compare the American clipper ship to the Basque canning vessel, the fragility of the Brazilian "jangada" to the robust fishing boats of Portugal.

Another of the museum's functions is development of an educational program for all those involved with things maritime, whether professionally or as an avocation. To these ends, the museum designs posters, edits books on the history and techniques of fishing, and develops plans for model makers, who by virtue of their passion for their craft are enthusiastic promoters of the museum.

The administration of the museum is directed by a staff of seven employees who are responsible for all aspects of its management. The museum benefits from the devotion and passion of this staff but recognizes that some moments are less agreeable than others. The museum has succeeded in relieving these occasional moments of difficulty and tension by providing the staff with a genuine fishing boat of its own, and it is not uncommon to run into the staff working at its most pleasurable activity—fishing on the Bay of Concarneau.

THE DEUTSCHES SCHIFFAHRTSMUSEUM, BREMERHAVEN

by Prof. Dr. D. Ellmers, Director in Charge

When the Deutsches Schiffahrtsmuseum was founded in 1971, it had immediate appeal to the public for two basic reasons. First is the fact that it is a combination of open-air museum, museum collection, and institute for scientific research. Second is its location, on a narrow peninsula between the Weser River, the North Sea, and the Old Dock, which in 1827 had been dug as an outport for Bremen. It became the nucleus of the town of Bremerhaven, gave it its name (Bremerhaven means "port of Bremen"), and is now the museum's dock with eight ships afloat, jetties and quays, dock-side cranes, and bascule bridges. Historical monuments from the early phase of maritime industrialization, such as lighthouses, locks, warehouses, and the first railway connection of a German seaport, most of them still working, stand along the city's waterfront. The mouth of the Weser River is a thoroughfare of inland vessels as well as for oceangoing ships; the latter change their pilots (river pilots for sea pilots) just in front of the musuem.

The Deutsches Schiffahrtsmuseum is thus embedded among the busy activities of a harbour town, and the famous German architect Hans Scharoun (1893-1972) designed the main building in such a way that this atmosphere is part of the display. These exhibitions give a complete survey of the maritime history of Germany, including the history of traffic along the big rivers, as they served as transcontinental lines of transport.

The world's oldest known archaeological remnant of a boat is a fragment of the rib of a skinboat that was excavated at Husum near the North Sea coast of northern Germany. The rib was carved from reindeer antler and has been dated to the last phase of the Ice Age (9000-8000 B.C.), at which time people lived from hunting reindeer near the glaciers. Pine and birch were the only trees, but they grew stunted and small and would not have suggested the idea of making logboats. In spite of their complicated construction, only skinboats could have been the earliest boats in the history of man, at least in middle and northern Europe, where rock carvings, done by reindeer hunters, give the oldest information on

Opposite: *Bird's-eye view of the Deutsches Schiffahrtsmuseum. In addition to the exhibitions and the vessels, the museum offers visitors an opportunity to participate in many activities, such as guided tours, educational programs, evening lectures, and participation in film competitions. In addition, amateur captains may maneuver scale models in the water by remote control or look through a submarine periscope.*

Above: *Late Paleolithic skinboat, 9000–8000 B.C.. (Photo by Egbert Laska)*

this type of boat. In order to use the rib from Husum in a full cross-section, these rock carvings and the methods employed today by Eskimos in making skinboats were studied, and the resulting information enabled the Deutsches Schiffahrtsmuseum to make a replica of the earliest type of boat, using nothing but the tools and materials available to those reindeer hunters. Nicely shaped arrows from pine had been excavated from digs dating back to the culture·that made the boat. Therefore it was decided to make all the wooden parts of the reconstruction from pine, but this first trial replica collapsed. Pine was far too brittle. The second replica was given a skeleton of birch and reindeer antler, and it proved to be a very sturdy, lightweight boat.

The essential tool for making watertight boats from the skins of reindeer is the sewing needle carved from reindeer antler. The earliest such sewing needles thus far known were excavated from layers of about 16000 B.C. Surprisingly enough, found in the same layers are the earliest fishing tools (fishing spears, fishing lines, and, from a later period, a fishing net). Obviously, by 16000 B.C., the reindeer hunters were much more interested in getting food out of the water than they had been before, when they had only their hands to catch it with. At this stage of their development, it was only a matter of time before they got enough experience with the sewing needle to make watertight seams. With this knowledge, they were able to construct the first skinboat sometime after 16000 B.C., enabling them to carry their fishing tools to every point on the surface of lakes, rivers, and coastal seas, thus making their fishing more effective. This then was the start of shipping, at least in this region of Germany.

Above: *Glass case with models of cargo vessels from the late 19th century. (Photo by Egbert Laska)*

Opposite, top: *Bronze ram of a Roman galley, ca. 10 B.C. (Photo by Egbert Laska)*

Opposite, bottom: *Hanseatic cog of Bremen, 1380.*

Thousands of years later, in the middle of the first century B.C., Julius Caesar had conquered what is today France, and the Rhine River became the borderline of the Roman Empire against Germanic tribes farther east and north. To protect this frontier, the emperor Augustus, toward the end of that century, established a navy of galleys on the Rhine with a naval base near Cologne. There is much pictorial evidence for the use of battering rams on ancient galleys, but only three original rams have thus far been excavated. One of them is the bronze ram of a Roman river galley in the Deutsches Schiffahrtsmuseum. The Roman sailors would use this ram to smash in the side of an enemy ship. For about four hundred years, the Roman river navy defended the Rhenish border. Later, Germanic tribes invaded France, the empire fell, and the Middle Ages began.

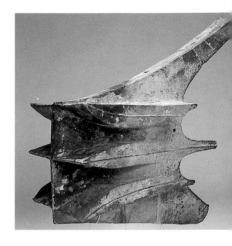

During the Middle Ages—in A.D. 1159—German merchants founded the port of Lubeck as a new window on the Baltic. These merchants formed the Hanseatic League, which in a short time dominated from Lubeck trade in the Baltic and North Sea. This domination lasted more than four centuries. During the first centuries, great use was made of the famous cargo vessel known as the Hanseatic cog. The first nearly complete hull of this type of vessel was excavated in the Weser River near Bremen during the years 1962 to 1965 and is now the museum's most outstanding exhibit. The ship had to be dismantled, and the museum's staff began in 1972 to reassemble the more than 2,000 broken pieces of this three-

dimensional jigsaw puzzle. After seven years of hard work, the complete cog was seen again, just as she was when she was launched in the autumn of 1379. The ship had not been fully outfitted, and melting ice in the early spring of 1380 caused a high water that pulled her from her berth, and since she had no ballast stone she capsized, was pressed down into the mud, and silted up.

The 23.23-meter-long cog is not longer than the big Viking ships, but is wider (7.62 meters), and its sides are much higher (4.26 meters), resulting in a cargo capacity of about eighty tons. She was the first type of ship with a stern rudder and with a real cabin beneath the castle deck, and had the first toilet as part of the cabin.

After the discovery of America by Columbus, Hanseatic merchants did not participate in transatlantic trade. Their longest voyages in the 16th century brought them to Lisbon in Portugal, from where they carried spices and other Indian and American goods to Germany. But when Dutch sailors began whaling in the Arctic during the 17th and 18th centuries, German whaling companies took part, too. The three-masted sailing vessels of these companies made what were then the longest regular voyages of German ships. The German whaling captains grew wealthy and invested their money in the Dutch style of comfortable living, with living rooms covered with Dutch tiles showing scenes from the Bible, the kind of scenes these men, with their hard and dangerous lives, preferred. Scriptural subjects also

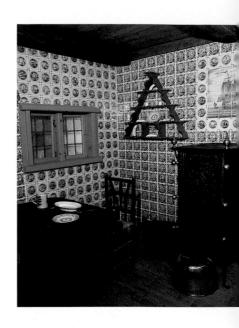

appear on the cast-iron "Bilegger" stoves, which were heated from an adjacent room. A special feature was a tableaux of ships made of sixteen individual Dutch tiles placed above a "Bilegger" stove.

For German shipping, the establishment of American independence in 1783 was an important event, and German merchants were quick to establish commercial relationships with the new nation. Their three-masted wooden sailing vessels carried emigrants to America and brought back American raw materials, such as cotton, tobacco, rice, and coffee, which became the base for industries in the port of Bremen. American merchants participated in that prosperous trade, and American shipwrights improved the wooden sailing ships by constructing the fast clipper ships in the middle of the 19th century. German shipwrights learned from them and made wooden and later iron sailing vessels in the clipper shape. One of the last oceangoing wooden sailing vessels in the clipper shape is the bark *Seute Deern* ("Sweet Girl"), now in the museum dock. She was built in 1919 at Gulfport, Mississippi, and nineteen years later came under the German flag as a cargo-carrying training vessel for the timber trade in the Baltic. When she got her last berth in the Old Dock of Bremerhaven in 1966, people liked her so much she became the nucleus for the Deutsches Schiffahrtsmuseum, which has become famous for its many different types of original German boats and ships.

Opposite: *Living quarters of a whaler captain, 1780. (Photo by Egbert Laska)*

Below: *Lightship* Elbe III, *1909, with a portion of her sails visible, in the museum's dock. (Photo by Egbert Laska)*

Following pages: *Wooden bark* Seute Deern, *1919. (Photo by Egbert Laska)*

One of the newest additions to the fleet in the museum's dock is the U-boat *Wilhelm Bauer* (U 2540), which leads us into the darkest period of modern German history, the reign of Hitler and World War II. Trying to cut off the British Isles from supply, Germany employed submarines to sink merchant ships. By the spring of 1943, using new means of detection and attack, the Allies were able to control the number of merchant ships being sunk, and the German submarine war was nearly defeated. With a completely new type of boat, namely the type XXI, the German U-boat command hoped once more to gain the advantage in the decisive area of tonnage sunk. But that was not to be, and the war ended before even one U-boat of the new type fired a torpedo at the enemy. Following the occupation of German shipyards, Allied naval specialists discovered the type XXI boats, the most advanced submarines in the world since they were capable of traveling submerged continuously. The last remaining boat of this type was used as a training ship in the navy of the Federal Republic of Germany until 1982, when it was converted into a floating museum. Visitors can study in detail all the technical arrangements that made this submarine so advanced for its time.

By exhibiting four dozen ships and boats in their actual size and more than 500 models in reduced scale, the Deutsches Schiffahrtsmuseum demonstrates German history

Above: *The paddle-steamer* Meissen, *1881, looms in the foreground in the galleries of the main building. (Photo by Egbert Laska)*

Below: *U-Boat type XXI* Wilhelm Bauer, *1945. (Photo by Egbert Laska)*

from the beginning in prehistory to the present time. Life and labor on board, in the ship-yards, and on the docks comes alive through the collections of small objects such as tools, arms, fancywork, dinner services from passenger-steamers as well as pottery from small sailing vessels, souvenirs from foreign ports, sea charts and nautical instruments, navy decorations and yachting prizes, fishing gear and ships' bells, figureheads and flags.

In addition to the permanent exhibitions in the open-air part of the museum, the main building and boat hall feature four or five temporary exhibitions each year that center on special topics of German or foreign maritime history. The library contains 50,000 volumes on German maritime history as well as archives of drawings and charts, photographs, posters, and ships' papers. The archaeological department has a laboratory for research in the conservation of waterlogged wood and, finally, there are field services working on inventories of technical monuments related to seafaring and of small craft along the shores and rivers of Germany.

From the earliest Husum skinboat to the reconstructed Hanseatic cog, from the elegant Mississippi clipper *Seute Deern* to the illustrious U-boat *Wilhelm Bauer*, the Deutsches Schiffahrtsmuseum preserves and narrates Germany's multifaceted maritime history.

Following pages: *The small sailing vessel* Groenland *was the ship of the first German Polar research expedition in 1868. She is in such good condition that every summer she leaves her berth with a museum crew aboard to conduct sailing tours in the North Sea and the Baltic.*

THE YOKOHAMA MARITIME MUSEUM, MEMORIAL FOUNDATION OF SAIL TRAINING SHIP *NIPPON MARU*, YOKOHAMA

by Jun Yoshino, Director, and Stephan K. Matsuo, Translator

The second largest city in Japan, with a population of 3.3 million, the port city of Yokohama sprawls relatively flat, its highest point a hill 150 meters in altitude. The name *Yokohama* translates literally as "sideways beach." The city is about thirty minutes by rail from Tokyo, the Keihin industrial belt lines its waterfront, and the city center faces Tokyo Bay. The temperate climate is touched by the four seasons.

A city name recognized throughout the world, Yokohama began its days in commerce when Japan opened her doors to the world with the 1854 Treaty of Peace, Amity and Commerce (often called the Treaty of Kanagawa). The signing of the U.S.-Japan Treaty of Amity and Commerce in 1858 was followed by separate treaties with Russia, the Netherlands, Great Britain, and France. On July 1, 1859, Yokohama was declared the first open port of Japan, and the city flourished. This date is now an annual day of celebration.

The cause behind all this was the arrival of the American naval officer Matthew Perry's squadron in 1853 and 1854 with the mission of opening Japan's doors to world trade. When Perry's so-called Black Ships called on this port, they awakened and began the transformation of both Yokohama and Japan. In the 130 years since, the city has survived the great Kanto earthquake, the destruction of World War II, and the postwar days of confiscation.

The year 1989 was both the one-hundred-thirtieth anniversary of Yokohama Port as well as the one-hundredth anniversary of the city's incorporation. In celebration, the city undertook an aggressive waterfront redevelopment program known as the Minato Mirai 21 ("Future of the Port 21st Century"), keynoting the plan with the Yokohama Exotic Showcase

Opposite: *Sail Training Ship* Nippon Maru *with sails set. Normally, the sails are kept furled, but once a month, except in the winter, volunteers unfurl her sails.*

Above: *The fan-shaped structure enfolding the Sail Training Ship* Nippon Maru *is the Yokohama Maritime Museum. To maximize the harbor view of the* Nippon Maru's *graceful lines, a large part of the museum is built underground. People can relax near the gentle, sloping roof, which blends into the waterfront. The ship is berthed at the No. 1 dock of the Yokohama Dock Company (soon to be the Mitsubishi Industries Company Yokohama Shipyard,) which dates back to 1899 and was created for construction of shipping vessels.*

Detail from a scroll showing the visit of Commodore Perry's visit to Japan ca. 1860–70. After 250 years of the Edo period during which the Japanese lived in relative isolation, the arrival of Commodore Perry's ships was a spectacular event. News of the arrival came to many people from tile engravings or pictures painted on scrolls such as this one which is 7-meters long. Perry's flagship, Powhaten has dropped anchor in the center of the harbor. To the rear is another Black Ship, the Saratoga. Smaller craft were used to shuttle Perry and his entourage to conference meetings in Yokohama to negotiate opening Japan's door for trade.

ホウハタン
長ヶ四十五間
幅濶処十三間許

Fair ("YES '89"), part of which was the opening of the Yokohama Maritime Museum on March 25.

Along with the Sail Training Ship *Nippon Maru*, the museum and the surrounding park occupy about 5.5 hectares (13.591 acres) and are known as the *Nippon Maru* Memorial Park. The museum, park, and ship are maintained by the Memorial Foundation of the Sail Training Ship *Nippon Maru*, organized through the auspices of Yokohama City.

Ten cities, including Tokyo and Kobe, submitted plans on how best to preserve the *Nippon Maru* and present her to the public, and the Tokyo Ministry of Transport Institute of Sea Training ultimately decided to entrust the care of the ship to Yokohama. She is now the city's symbol.

At the same time, a "Report on Future Plans" was prepared by the Yokohama Marine Science Museum and submitted to the office of the mayor of Yokohama. In celebration of the one-hundredth anniversary of the port in 1959, this museum had exhibited maritime artifacts on the third floor of the 108-meter Yokohama Marine Tower, but as time passed it became increasingly apparent that a better-suited location was needed to house the exhibits. Visions of a Yokohama Maritime Museum thus began to take shape in 1986.

Only a year earlier, in April 1985, public display of the *Nippon Maru* had begun. A four-masted barque (97 meters in length with a weight of 2,278 metric tons), the *Nippon Maru* had been used since 1930 as a training vessel. During the ensuing fifty-four years, including the period of World War II, roughly 11,500 seamen were trained on the ship. The ship's voyages have taken her the equivalent of forty-five and one-half times around the world, a record for a sailing ship. She is berthed at the No. 1 dock of the Yokohama Dock Company (soon to be the Mitsubishi Industries Company Yokohama Shipyard), which dates back to 1899 and is the oldest extant facility. No changes have been made to the *Nippon Maru*, so the ship is presented in its original form.

The Ooka River flows past the museum, which is adjacent to the No. 1 dock. Most of the museum is underground to best display the *Nippon Maru*. Construction began in December 1986, and was completed in October 1988. To protect the building from water, it is surrounded by a wall of reinforced concrete 400 meters long, 80 centimeters thick, and 13 meters deep. Almost 70,000 cubic meters of earth were excavated. The building totals 7,145 square meters, the lower floor alone being some 4,800 meters. At a depth of more than 10 meters, the museum is unique—no other museums are engineered in a way similar to this facility.

From the air, one can see the *Nippon Maru* and the open space near it. The museum's roof is a gentle lawnlike slope toward the river's edge, and people can be seen relaxing near the water. The upper floor of the museum has a lobby, museum shop, restaurant, and exhibition hall. The underground lower main floor is exceptionally spacious, housing the exhibits in the central area, with additional space provided for special exhibitions and a library.

The theme of the museum is the creation of a window view of modern Japan focus-

The Pier of Yokohama.　　横濱棧橋ノ入口

Above: *Unloading tea at the wharf of the tea manufacturer, No. 14, 1885; woodblock print. Employees of the tea manufacturer, the Oukoku Company, readying the domestically produced tea for the long sea voyage.*

Left: *Hand-colored postcard, "The Pier of Yokohama," ca. 1900-10. As the quality of photographic papers advanced, postcards were hand-colored after enlargement and made into albums. Yokohama had about ten companies making these postcards which depicted port and town scenes and often showed sightseers looking at the ships near the Osanbashi pier.*

ing on the harbor and port activities and their relationship with the world. The exhibits are divided into five main sections: the role of sailing vessels such as the Sail Training Ship *Nippon Maru*; the "History of the Port of Yokohama" from "open door" to present-day Japan; "Scenes from the Port of Yokohama," with three cameras sending live television pictures; "Ships in Transition," with development of the ships of the 19th century to the present day; and "Ports throughout the World," with exhibits and views of sister ports to Yokohama and others. Along with special displays, computerized images and other new techniques are utilized. The library has a collection of maps pertaining to the oceans and is augmented by file collections and video tapes.

Blowing black smoke and cutting relentlessly through the sea, the Black Ships of Perry's squadron were overwhelming to the Japanese. This, the first encounter with western civilization, signaled the downturn of the political system of the Tokugawa government. In this crisis, however uneasy the mood of the people, there was also curiosity. Scrolls and woodblock prints then served as newspapers, and these spread news of the event and became known as the "Black Ship scrolls." Thus were appetites whetted and curiosity aroused.

As Yokohama became an open port, it came to encompass a customs house, wharf, credit office, roads, bridges, and more. To the east of the customs house was a European settlement, and to the west, residences of the local population. As the number of people involved in the export trade increased, so did the amount of settlement trade. Imports of cotton and woolen goods gave way to machinery and steel goods, while the major export was raw silk. The trade in silk reached fervent levels, and the number of traders increased accordingly. Tomitaro Hara, under the name "Sankei," was notably outstanding. Financing a silk thread factory, he became a central figure in the Yokohama financial community. Hara removed several old buildings and privately financed and created a Japanese garden in the space known as the Sankei-en. This park still exists and is a place where one can go to relax. Tea followed raw silk as a major export commodity, particularly to the United States. As with silk, the tea trade led to the formation of merchant handlers, each with its own unique label from multicolored woodblock prints, complete with brand name, tea type, distribution company name, and the words "Japan Tea." During this period, the port of Yokohama handled two-thirds of all trade in Japan.

Many foreign consulates and trading houses began establishing themselves in Yokohama and had a decided effect on the city's culture. The presence of foreigners, their cultures and everyday life, and scenes of foreign ships were depicted on colorful woodblock prints known as Yokohama *ukiyo-e*. As tourist souvenirs, as well as informative sheets on local companies, these prints caught on with explosive popularity. Entry into the foreign settlement was rigidly controlled, and while some of the stories told on the prints were obviously fiction, they offered a fascinating glimpse of a totally different world. Many Yokohama *ukiyo-e* were printed, and a few remain that depict the waterfront and the handling of cargo. These were important ways of informing merchants of events.

Above, top: *Model of Edo-period sailing ship* Benzai-sen. *Named for its cargo of rice bales and the money earned from hauling this cargo, this vessel was known as a "sengoku-bune" or "1,000 bales of rice boat." Primarily used in the Inland Sea, the boat combined both sail and oar until the Edo period, when design improvements allowed her to move more swiftly by sail alone. The new style enabled her to carry 2,000 bales of rice—twice her former load.*

Above, middle: *Model of the passenger ship* Kamakura Maru, *1930-43, which was used on sea routes east to San Francisco and was the largest Japanese passenger ship prior to World War II. Built as the* Chichibu Maru *at the No. 1 Dock facility, she was renamed as the* Kamakura Maru *in 1938 when she was requisitioned for service in World War II and subsequently sunk in action.*

Above, bottom: *Model of the cargo-passenger ship* Argentina Maru, *1939-48, built by the Osaka Kaisha to transport emigrants to South America and for use as a Yokohama-based passenger ship for round-the-world routes. Although resources were difficult to obtain during that era, her fittings were of excellent quality. The ship's levels were tiered like stairs, and the smokestack was of a new circular form. The decking was also matched in a circular parquet. She was requisitioned during World War II, renamed the* Kaiyo, *and refitted as an aircraft carrier.*

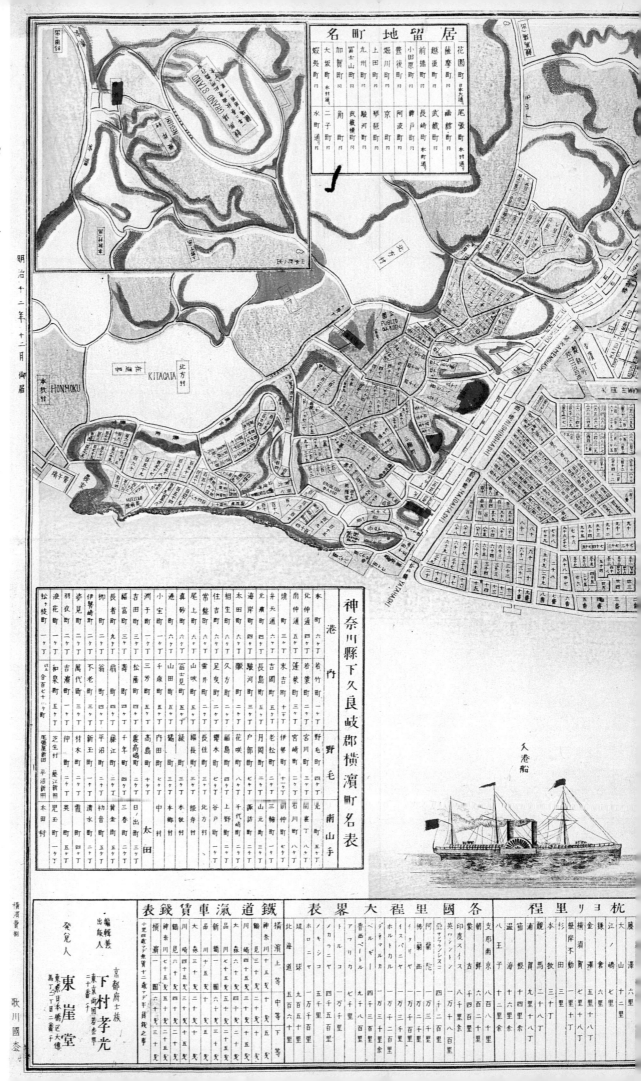

Detailed map of Yokohama, 1879. Copperplate printed and then rich colors added by consecutive woodblock printing in a style reminiscent of ukiyo-e. The large trade wharf is visible in the center. To its left is the area where foreigners settled. Chinatown is located where a cluster of roads radiates from the perpendicular lines. The hilly area following the coast is Yamate, home to another settlement of foreigners. The origins of modern Yokohama can be seen from the location of the railway station, lighthouse, customs, prefectural government buildings, park, steel mill, race track, and other details on the map.

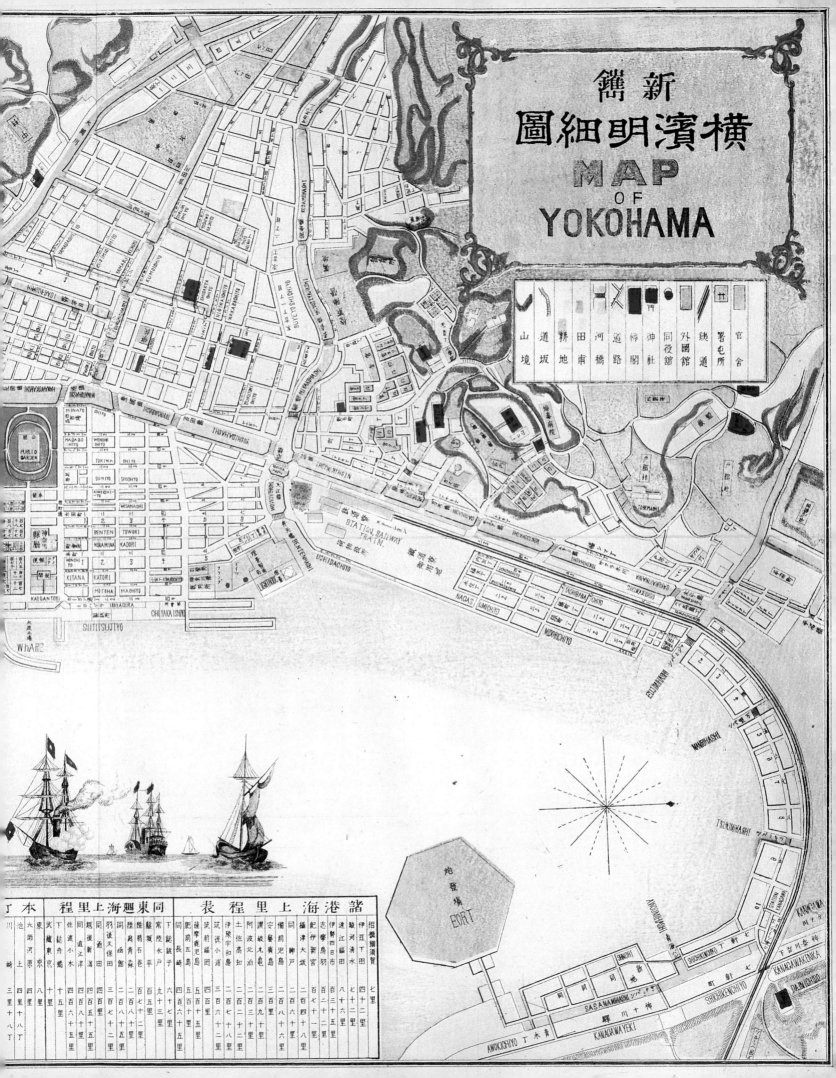

新鐫
横濱明細圖
MAP
OF
YOKOHAMA

As the volume of trade increased, so too did the number of ships entering Yokohama. However, the facilities of the port were poor, as is revealed by an examination of the "Detailed Map of Yokohama." Most ships dropped anchor offshore, and small barges laden with cargo would ferry between the ships and the shore. Plans to build pier facilities were initiated. Finally, in 1898, two seawalls and a mooring facility (today known as the Osanbashi Pier) were completed. Next, in 1916, a pier complete with a crane that customs could use as facilities (today's Shinko Pier) was made available. By the 1900s, European and American companies with interests in Yokohama numbered eighteen, with more than 201 scheduled ships. Japanese ships also began going abroad. Most of the trade routes overseas began in the port of Yokohama. The Toyo Kisen Company's ship *Tenyo Maru* (13,454 metric tons) became the leading passenger ship of Japan.

The shipping and shipbuilding industries became important and grew despite the political, economic, or corporate policies of the period. Wars augmented ship movement and expansion. Interspersed within the history of Japanese commercial shipping were the Sino-Japanese War, the Russo-Japanese War, and World War I. Japanese shipping then ranked third after Great Britain and the United States. However, in World War II, extensive damage was wrought on the industry. This museum seeks to preserve the modern-day history of the ships that took part in that history. Of these, three large scale models are exhibited: the *Kamakura Maru*, the *Argentina Maru*, and the *André Lebon*. Each model measures some three meters in length.

The *André Lebon* (13,682 metric tons) set sail in 1919 from Marseilles destined for Yokohama. The cargo passenger ship belonged to the French Messageries Maritime Company. On the day of the Great Kanto Earthquake, September 1, 1923, in a few moments Yokohama was all but destroyed. At that time, the *André Lebon* was berthed at the Osanbashi Pier along with Canadian Pacific's *Empress of Australia*. Quake victims were taken aboard the *André Lebon* and given shelter. To the citizens of Yokohama, *André Lebon* is a name not easily forgotten. Within the museum collection is a model of the ship, presented to this museum's predecessor, the Yokohama Marine Science Museum, as a memento by the Messageries Maritime Company.

The museum is built on the spot where the Yokohama Dock Company had its warehouse. The *Kamakura Maru* (17,498 metric tons) was built in 1930 at this No. 1 dock facility. At the time of her launching, she was named *Chichibu Maru* and was used on the Tokyo-San Francisco route. Before World War II, the ship was Japan's largest passenger ship. Her owners were the Osaka Shosen Company and the Nippon Yusen Company. This was during the glory days of cargo passenger ships, and the *Chichibu Maru* had fittings and service that rivaled those of American and English ships. Refitted for use in the Pacific War, and renamed at that time, the *Kamakura Maru* was sunk.

In 1939, the *Argentina Maru* (12,759 metric tons) was fitted as a round-the-world ship by way of South America. Three years after the beginning of World War II, she was refit-

ted as an aircraft carrier and christened *Kaiyo*. Her owners, the Osaka Shosen Company, had established a branch office in Buenos Aires, and a decorative model of the ship was made from actual scale plans. When the office was closed with wartime hostilities, the model was kept by the chairman of the Japanese Association and was then displayed at the Argentine National Nautical School. When this museum opened, the school and the Mitsui OSK Lines presented the museum with the model, and after fifty years abroad it was finally returned to Japan.

Other ship models from the postwar period used in the Japanese transport industry, including general cargo ships, container ships, and motor vehicle transports, are on display. Major acquisition items include port charts, navigation instruments, ship layouts, shipbuilding tools, oceanographic charts, ship models, passenger ship posters, ship fittings, postcards, and photographs. The library contains items of interest for all, from youngsters to professionals, and with its 9,000 holdings is an important research source. Special model-making sessions, observations of ports and ships, films and lectures in the "cinetalk" program, and ship tours are all part of the summer vacation programs of the museum.

The primary focus of the Yokohama Maritime Museum will continue to center on the 130-year history of Yokohama as a port as well as on Japan's recent transport and shipbuilding industries, and the museum intends to continue documenting Japan's rich maritime patrimony.

NETHERLANDS

THE NEDERLANDS SCHEEPVAART MUSEUM, AMSTERDAM

by Willem F. J. Mörzer Bruyns, Head Curator

The kingdom of the Netherlands is situated on the southeastern border of the North Sea. The country can be roughly divided into two parts, one of which lies above and one of which lies at or below sea level. The northern and western part of the country, comprising the provinces of Groningen, Friesland, North and South Holland, and Zeeland, share the 800-kilometer-long coastline. The shape of the coastline has remained roughly the same over the centuries. In prehistoric times, the many arms of the sea in the present-day province of Zeeland did not exist, and only a relatively small lake was in the center of the country. From 57 B.C. to A.D. 400 the northern border of the Roman Empire was formed by the Rhine River and its tributaries. Roman settlements existed along the banks of these rivers, and ample evidence of shipping activity, limited to river and coastal trade, has been found. Around 800, Norsemen, arriving in longboats, settled in the Low Countries. Still later, large floods created an inland sea, named the Zuiderzee, in the heart of the country. Merchants in North Sea and Zuiderzee ports traded for products not available in the Netherlands with ports in other countries bordering the North Sea, the Baltic, the English Channel, the Bay of Biscay, and the Mediterranean. Zuiderzee cities like Stavoren and Kampen traded with other Hanseatic League ports and, for a period, enjoyed great prosperity.

During the 16th century some of these ports lost their importance, while others, like the city of Dordrecht, to the southeast of Rotterdam, and Middelburg, became important or retained their status. In the 16th century, Enkhuizen and Amsterdam became increasingly important and wealthy. Even so, maritime trade did not extend beyond European waters. Evidence of the limited range can be found in the early printed "rutters of the sea," sailing guides for the North Sea, the Channel, and the Baltic. One of the most important events of 16th-century maritime cartography was the publication in 1584 of the *Spieghel der Zeevaerdt,* by Lucas Janszoon Waghenaer of Enckhuysen. This was the first maritime atlas, a combination of sea charts and written sailing directions. It was soon translated into English,

Opposite: *Celestial globe dated 1613 made by Amsterdam cartographers Jodocus Hondius and Adriaan Veen. Globes like this were used aboard ships to identify the constellations and on land for educational purposes.*

Above: *View of the Lands Zeemagazijn, built in 1656 on 18,000 piles, as a storehouse and arsenal for the ships of the Admiralty of Amsterdam. Designed by the Amsterdam city architect Daniel Stalpaert, the building has been the home of the Nederlands Scheepvaart Museum since 1973.*

Following pages: A Dutch Roadstead with Venetian Merchantman (left) and Dutch Ships. *Oil painting on canvas by A. Willaerts, 1627. Before Dutch dominance at sea was established, the Venetians transported merchandise from the Mediterranean to the southern Netherlands.*

French, and German. Only a short time later, the Dutch began their maritime expansion beyond European waters.

During the 14th and 15th centuries, virtually all the Low Countries were controlled by the dukes of Burgundy. Mary of Burgundy's marriage to Archduke Maximilian (later Emperor Maximilian I) brought the Low Countries into the house of Hapsburg. In 1555, Emperor Charles V gave them to his son Philip II of Spain, making them part of the Spanish Hapsburg Empire. The struggle for religious freedom led to a revolt against Philip II and an eighty-year war for independence. The republic of the United Provinces, as the young nation called itself, soon challenged Spanish and Portuguese supremacy at sea to become the world's leading maritime nation. The city of Amsterdam was the focal point in that effort. Following a fourteen-month siege, Spanish Catholic armies seized the city of Antwerp in 1585. The Dutch then blockaded the Scheldt River, making shipping to and from that port impossible for the next two hundred years. Antwerp declined rapidly, leading to an exodus of merchants, scientists, and intellectuals, a great many of whom settled in Amsterdam, which thus received the impetus to expand economically and extend its area of trade beyond European borders.

A vital figure in the first Dutch expeditions to Asia, and the man instrumental in finding the route, was the Reverend Petrus Plancius (1552-1622), an immigrant from Antwerp. An eminent geographer and author of maps and charts essential to establishing the route to the Orient, Plancius collaborated with the Amsterdam publisher Cornelis Claes and was able to obtain secret cartographical information on Asian sailing routes from a Spanish navigator.

In 1595, the Dutch equipped their first expedition from Amsterdam to Asia by way of the Cape of Good Hope. The objective was establishment of a direct spice trade with the Orient that would avoid dealing with the Portuguese, who had discovered the route to the east a hundred years earlier. This goal was a logical consequence of intense Dutch seafaring in European waters.

Also during the 1590s, the Dutch equipped three expeditions in search of the Northeast Passage, a route north of Russia to Asia. This, of course, was not found, but it led to the discovery of the wealth of seals and whales in the Arctic region. A prosperous whaling industry was soon set up around the Arctic islands of Jan Mayen and Spitsbergen. From then on, whale-oil lamps burned in Dutch houses. Along with the much older herring industry, whaling brought wealth to ports like Enkhuizen, De Rijp, and, of course, Amsterdam.

With the help of the charts Plancius had obtained from Spain and the knowledge of Jan Huygen van Linschoten, the route to the East Indies by way of the Cape of Good Hope was found. Van Linschoten had worked in the service of the Bishop of Goa for many years and had made notes on navigation and trade that he published under the title *Itinerario*.

After several successful trading expeditions to the East Indies, the Dutch United East India Company was founded in 1602. This became a large and wealthy enterprise, obtaining from the Netherlands States-General a monopoly on trade with areas east of the Cape of Good Hope and west of the Strait of Magellan. Ships in the service of the company were the

Opposite, top: *A tile tableau, ca. 1919, depicting the S.S.* Leersum *behind the Amsterdam Central Station. The* Leersum *belonged to the Stoomvaart Mij "Oostzee," an Amsterdam tramping company. The tableau commemorates the 1914-19 cooperation of that company and an English firm.*

Opposite, bottom left: *An 18th-century glass with engraved scenes of a whale hunt by the whaler* Hollandia, *under Commander Willem van der Keuken.*

Opposite, bottom right: *Model of the* Maaslloyd, *a general cargo vessel built in the early 1950s for the Royal Rotterdam Lloyd. Ships like the* Maaslloyd, *built for the trade between the Netherlands and Indonesia, eventually sailed to ports all over the world.*

Following pages: *Return of the* Hollandia *to the Roadstead of Texel in 1665 with Lieutenant Admiral-General Michiel de Ruyter (1607-76). Oil painting on canvas by Ludolph Bakhuizen. The* Hollandia *became de Ruyter's flagship shortly after his appointment as Commander-in-Chief of the combined fleet of the Dutch Admiralties.*

first to reach Australia, in 1606. From its headquarters at Batavia (founded in 1619), the company set up trading posts on the island of Formosa in 1624, and in Japan in 1641. The company remained in operation until the end of the 18th century.

Dutch maritime expansion was not limited to the Orient and the Arctic. The English navigator Henry Hudson, engaged in 1609 by the East India Company to find the Northeast Passage, sailed to Spitsbergen. Finding his way blocked by ice and cold, and facing a mutinous crew, he disobeyed his orders and headed west to North America to seek out the Northwest Passage. He thus discovered what is now the Hudson River, an event that eventually led to the founding of the Dutch West Indies Company in 1621. This company established settlements in Brazil in 1624, on Manhattan Island in 1625, and on Tobago in the West Indies in 1628, all the while being attacked and harassed by the Spanish and Portuguese. The decline of the Spanish and Portuguese as competitive sea powers left only the English as serious economic opponents of the Dutch. This fierce competition resulted in the two Dutch Wars, fought from 1652 to 1654 and from 1664 to 1667.

Fought mainly at sea, these wars bred highly skillful admirals. Such men as Michiel

Adriaanszoon de Ruyter, Maarten Harpertszoon Tromp and his son Cornelis Tromp, Isaac Sweers, Jan Evertsen, and Jacob van Wassenaer Obdam made lasting names for themselves. Portraits of these admirals, paintings of the battles they fought, and models of the ships they sailed in can be seen in the Nederlands Scheepvaart Museum in Amsterdam.

This museum is the result of cooperation between a private museum enterprise and the Netherlands government. The Nederlandsch Historisch Scheepvaart Museum in Amsterdam, financed by private money, opened its doors to the public in 1922 in a small building. Its collection was enlarged through active acquisition over the years by wealthy collectors and enthusiastic amateurs.

At the beginning of the 20th century, historical maritime objects were readily available and relatively inexpensive. Most museums were not particularly interested in maritime artifacts, and the 19th century was not of primary interest to museum curators.

During the second decade of this century, the money available for financing the museum came from shipping companies, shipbuilding firms, banks, merchant houses, and insurance companies. Merchant shipping had done reasonably well for the economy of the neutral Netherlands during the Great War.

Besides money, artifacts were donated by individuals from all over the country, by shipping companies and other maritime enterprises, and by the Royal Netherlands Navy. Top-quality artifacts were brought in by private collectors. One of the first to donate his collection to the museum was the wealthy Amsterdam merchant G. C. E. Crone, in 1919. The Crone family had made its fortune in the previous centuries with the spice trade. Their collection consisted of contemporary ship models dating from the 17th to 19th centuries.

In 1921, Anton Mensing, director of Frederik Muller & Company Auctioneers in Amsterdam, sold the museum his prints, drawings, maps, charts, and large library. The library contained a number of early atlases and Dutch travel books, laying the basis for one of the most important libraries of its kind in the world.

Shortly before the museum opened in 1922, the Dutch national museum, the Rijksmuseum in Amsterdam, lent a collection of maritime historical objects from its Dutch history department. That same year the Amsterdam collector C. G. 't Hooft sold his prints, drawings, and contemporary ship models from the 17th to 19th centuries. In 1926, the model collection of the Meyjes family of Amsterdam shipbuilders, with pieces dating to the beginning of the 18th century, was presented to the museum.

As a result of the world economic crisis at the end of the 1920s and early 1930s, many private individuals could no longer afford to support the museum. Accumulated capital was devalued, yielding less interest. It was no longer possible to purchase objects of great value. An unfortunate conflict between one of the trustees and the museum resulted in the withdrawal of that trustee's large loan to the museum. The collection of Van de Velde drawings went to the National Maritime Museum in Greenwich. This museum, supported by the wealthy James Caird, was able to overbid on practically anything it wanted. In 1930, matters got worse when the Rijksmuseum withdrew its loan to refurbish its relevant department.

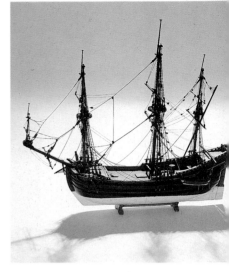

Opposite, top: An East Indiaman on "Camels" Being Towed across Pampus Shoal in the Mouth of the IJ before Amsterdam. *Watercolor by H. Kobell (1751-79). The ship is flying the Dutch East India Company (or Verenigde Oostindische Compagnie) flag. The storehouse of the company is visible in the background (left). Ships' "camels," a device similar to the present-day dry-dock, were constructed to lift ships with considerable draught over the Pampus Shoal.*

Opposite, bottom: *A silver bar retreived from the wreck of the Dutch East India Company ship* Slot ter Hooghe, *sunk in 1724. The company exported silver bullion to the Orient to finance the trade in spices and other expensive products.*

Above: *Model of whaler* Willem Prins van Oranje, *dated 1690. This model clearly shows the wide deck for processing whales. Across the poop deck is a heavy transverse beam that took the after tackle for hoisting and lowering the whale boats. This is one of the world's oldest models of a whaler.*

Despite these setbacks, the Nederlandsch Historisch Scheepvaart Museum managed to assemble one of the largest and most important maritime historical collections in the world during the first ten years of its existence, and the collecting continued. At the end of World War II, a library on the history of sea tactics belonging to the late Professor J. C. M. Warnsinck was acquired. In 1968, trustee Ernst Crone, cousin of G. C. E. Crone, donated his navigational instruments, and, after his death in 1976, his library of navigational manuals and books on the history of navigation followed.

Left: *Portrait of Admiral Cornelis Tromp (1629-91); Oil painting on canvas attributed to Sir Peter Lely, ca. 1677. At the age of 19, Tromp already commanded a small squadron. He fought in three Anglo-Dutch wars but was temporarily deprived of his command in 1666 at the insistence of Admiral-General Michiel de Ruyter.*

In 1968, the government decided to create a state-run maritime museum with the collection of the Nederlandsch Historisch Scheepvaart Museum as the cornerstone, and the museum's collection was moved from the small building to the spacious 17th-century Lands Zeemagazijn on the old Amsterdam waterfront.

The Zeemagazijn was built in 1656 as the arsenal for the Amsterdam Admiralty. It contained virtually everything necessary to equip Amsterdam's men-of-war, with supplies ranging from sails and ropes, weapons and flags, to food, water, and tar. The building burned down one night in 1791, leaving only the walls standing. After restoration work, the blackened brick walls were covered with plaster. The Admiralty was dissolved in 1796 as a result of political changes inspired by the French Revolution, and the Zeemagazijn became a storehouse for the Royal Netherlands Navy until 1973, when the museum took possession.

In 1975, the government's decision to create a national maritime museum came into effect. The trustees of the Nederlandsch Historisch Scheepvaart Museum put the collection on permanent loan to the state, which then financed the extensive restoration of the Lands Zeemagazijn. The refurbishing was completed in 1981, and the museum was officially opened.

Visitors today find a permanent exhibition on the history of Dutch shipping similar to but much more elaborate than the museum's exhibition in 1922, when it first opened to the public. Through twenty-five rooms the visitor follows exhibits on late medieval sea trade; 16th-century Dutch exploration; 17th-century trade with the East Indies, whaling and herring fishing, and the Anglo-Dutch wars; 18th-century innovations in shipbuilding, navigation, and armament; 19th-century steam propulsion and shipbuilding in iron, colonial trade, and yachting; and finally the 20th-century world wars, the Royal Barge of H. M. Queen Beatrix, and even the first Dutch-made wind surfer.

The museum owns three vessels moored along the building's jetty. They are a coal-fired icebreaker built in Amsterdam in 1900, a 1912 herring-lugger, and the first Dutch self-righting lifeboat, commissioned in 1924. Recently a scale 1:1 replica of the Dutch East Indiaman *Amsterdam* was moored alongside and can be visited by the public.

Each year, one large and two small temporary exhibitions are prepared around one of the museum's collections. The subjects range from maritime cartography and Arctic exploration to the history of yachting and Dutch 17th-century marine paintings. Scholars do research in the large library or consult the storeroom collections of paintings, prints, and drawings, the ship drafts and models, or the navigational instruments and sea charts. Indeed, the elegant complex of the Amsterdam Nederlands Scheepvaart Museum, which includes in its historical Zeemagazijn, facilities for meetings and conferences, a restaurant, a book and souvenir shop, and an extensive library as well as the twenty-five rooms of exhibits and the actual vessels moored at the jetty, provides a fitting forum to celebrate Dutch maritime history.

NETHERLANDS

THE MARITIEM MUSEUM
PRINS HENDRIK, ROTTERDAM

by Leo M. Akveld, Curator

The Netherlands. A country literally, as the phrase has it, wrested from the sea. Bordering the North Sea, of old one of the busiest shipping areas of the world. Intersected by a number of well navigable rivers that deeply penetrate the European hinterland. A country that has many times sought the mercantile or naval hegemony of the high seas. A country, today and in the past, full of people to whom ships and shipping are familiar phenomena; people who know how to value the importance of maritime activity in relation to the prosperity of their country; people who know their maritime heritage and who often admire their ancestors who have created that heritage.

Rotterdam. A late starter among the port cities of the Low Countries, but in the late 16th century already deriving large riches from the herring fishery. Soon afterward becoming a very busy and prosperous center of seagoing and inland navigation. Knowing many ups and downs, Rotterdam remained an important port city, while today it is the world's biggest port in terms of the quantity of goods that are yearly transshipped. In 1874, the Maritiem Museum Prins Hendrik was founded as a municipal museum—the oldest maritime museum in the Netherlands.

The man whom the museum is named after is Prince Hendrik (1820-79), the third son of King Willem II. Being a naval officer himself and an active protagonist of the Dutch merchant navy, Hendrik strived to encourage Dutch youngsters to enlist in the navy or the merchant marine. To accomplish this end, he founded the Rotterdam Royal Dutch Yacht Club in 1845 and became its first chairman. Using that yacht club, Hendrik hoped to excite interest with the Rotterdam youngsters in learning how to row and to sail, in that way encouraging them to choose a seafaring profession. He tried to arouse their curiosity for the Dutch maritime heritage also by founding a so-called model room in the yacht club building. In that exhibition mostly 19th-century ship models were on show, examples of ship decoration, models of the equipment and the rigging of such vessels—using often newly developed techniques—models of guns, and so on. In total, the collection of the yacht club's model room in 1873 included some 200 items.

Opposite: *Coca de Mataró, votive model, 15th century. At about the time that Columbus sailed to America and Magellan made his voyage around the world, the ship went through a phase of radical transition. Its size grew, new construction techniques were used, and rigging changed. Many paintings give us ideas about this time, but only one three-dimensional object remains— this 15th-century votive model of a Catalan merchantman, a rather slow sailing ship with a cargo capacity of about 85 tons, from a small church in Mataró, a village on the Mediterranean coast near Barcelona.*

Above: *Oak dug-out fish-box from 2nd century A.D. From thousands of rather amorphous pieces of wood, a fish-box is slowly emerging. Still embedded in sand, the small dug-out ship is gradually revealing the craftsmanship of a 2nd-century boatbuilder who lived on the banks of the Rhine somewhere in the swampy areas of the Low Countries.*

In 1874, the yacht club opened the doors of its model room to the general public. The model room thus became a maritime museum. When the yacht club was closed in 1880, the city government bought its premises. Until 1948, the museum remained in the former yacht club building on the banks of the Maas River, right in the heart of what was then the business center of Rotterdam. Although the building was not destroyed during the 1940 German bombardment of the city, the city government thought it wise to remove most of the museum's collections to a safe place outside the city. In 1948, the Prins Hendrik Museum moved into new premises, newly built and better equipped to fulfill the demands of a modern presentation of its collections. Above the entrance door of the museum an artist's impression of the 15th-century model of a Catalan merchantman, the "coca de Mataró," was installed. By then this famous model had become the museum's logo.

Late in the 1970s, the Rotterdam Maritime Museum lost its building again. It had to give way to the east-west tunnel of the subway system, then under construction near the

Above: Amsterdam Waterfront, *hand-colored engraving by Pieter Mortier, ca. 1700. Be careful when dealing with historical sources. That is what this engraving teaches us. Against the background of the Amsterdam waterfront, we see an official yacht carrying the standard of a prince of Orange. At the right, a Dutch man-of-war. So far so good. But what appear to be a number of golden tassels dangling in front of the bows of that ship—tassels which would seem merely to be part of the ship's decoration—are actually just ordinary brooms used to wipe off the human waste from the bows to diminish the stench below decks. The common sailors relieved themselves sitting on the headrails of the backhead.*

museum building. In 1987, a splendid new museum building was opened to the public. It stands in the heart of today's Rotterdam at the northern end of the Leuvehaven, one of the oldest harbor basins of the city, its history dating to the early 17th century. The new building was designed by the famous Dutch architect Wim Quist. He made a very spacious building, with a large number of huge glass windows on the ground floor that create a direct link between the heart of today's Rotterdam and the city's historic and modern lifeline, the Maas River. The building has a triangular form in which the exhibition floors, the storage room, and the offices have been accommodated. On the ground floor a large square box has been shoved into the base of the triangle; that exhibition room, covering 800 square meters and with a height of 4.5 meters, houses the permanent exhibition of the Prins Hendrik Museum, the "vade mecum."

From 1874 onward, the Rotterdam Maritime Museum had on show a chronologically ordered exhibition covering the whole of Dutch maritime history. Temporary exhibitions

Above: Portrait of a Dutch Merchantman, *grisaille, by Willem van de Velde the Elder, (ca. 1611-97) signed and dated 1648. Using a technique often practiced in the 17th century of showing the same ship from various angles, this master depicts a beautifully decorated and heavily armed ship, probably the* Mercurius, *a vessel that was chartered in 1653 by the Dutch East India Company and sunk in a battle with the English fleet that same year. The ship's elegant transom (left) and the beautifully curved line of its sheer (right) are apparent. Judging from the way she seems to sail directly towards the viewer (center), she seems to be a fast sailor.*

were regularly organized to highlight certain events or more general aspects of that history. Since 1987, however, the presentation of the Prins Hendrik Museum has been organized in another way. The permanent exhibition focuses on the everlasting elements of mankind's maritime history; on elements that can be found everywhere on earth at any given moment in history. These elements have been divided into two groups: the purposes of shipping—transport, exercise of power, gathering of food, geographic and oceanographic research, recreation, and such supporting activities as dredging and piloting; and the elements of shipping, those building stones necessary for the creation of every form of shipping—shipbuilding, ships, propulsion, harbors, shipping routes, shipping companies, crews, navigation, and maritime law.

Beginning with this analysis of maritime history, the Prins Hendrik Museum then offers temporary exhibitions. For these, the museum has at its disposal a large and rich collection, including all the kinds of objects to be found in any maritime museum. The collection of 1,400 ship models and half-models of vessels of all ages shows a certain emphasis on 19th- and 20th-century examples. There are also 240 navigational instruments, 150 examples of ship decoration, 300 atlases, 1,000 maps, 145,000 shipbuilders' plans, 80,000 documentary photographs, and so on.

The Prins Hendrik Maritime Museum also has in its collection a number of unique

Above: *Officer's mess room aboard the former turret-ram H.N.M.S.* Buffel, *1868. In times not so long ago, going to sea stood for leaving behind for many months everything that was dear to a seaman: relatives and a trusted living environment. To keep these memories alive even aboard a man-of-war, officers and common seamen decorated their quarters with scenes from home and portraits of relatives. The museum restored this atmosphere with comfortable leather benches, beautiful soft green colors, a piano, plants, paintings of woods, and a typical Dutch snowy polder-landscape.*

items. First of all, there is the contemporary model of a 15th-century Catalan merchantman, the so-called coca de Mataró. The model, a votive object once donated to a chapel in the mariners' village of Mataró on the Catalan coast near Barcelona, dates from a period in which the coastal vessel grew to a real oceangoing ship. It is unique in that it is the only three-dimensional depiction of a ship from an important transitional period in its development.

Left above: *Model of an IJsseltjalk by Jelle Hazenberg. During the late 19th- and early 20th-century rapid expansion of Rotterdam, its infrastructure needed modernization. Large dwelling areas were built. New harbor basins required modern quays. Railway embankments were constructed. Enormous quantities of sand and gravel were needed, and much of it came from the Hollandse IJssel. It was dredged by skippers from villages along that river and brought into Rotterdam on ships such as these. Like all Dutch vessels for inland navigation, they were flat-bottomed ships with leeboards, but characteristic of the IJsseltjalk were the elegant lines and the somewhat pronounced sheer, which is why they were sometimes called IJsselyachts. The brilliant colors of their hulls strengthened that impression.*

Left below: *Model of the herring lugger s'Gravenhage, 1892. The fisheries in the Netherlands maritime provinces experienced many ups and downs from the 16th century onwards. They have always been a very important economic factor. Very specialized ships were used, equipped to use huge drift nets that hung vertically in the water. Until the middle of the 19th century, the herring buss was the working platform of the herring fishermen. At that time, it was replaced by the lugger, which sailed faster and offered more working space. This model shows a number of the characteristics of a Dutch lugger. In the side, one can see the big rolls that were used to shoot and haul in the nets; behind them, the cribs into which the herring was shaken. From there, the fish was taken for gutting, salting, and packing layer upon layer into barrels which were stowed in the fish hold, the hatches of which can be seen amidships.*

Following pages: *Part of a map of Rotterdam, engraving by Romeyn de Hooghe, signed and dated 1694. Shown is the triangular heart of the port city at the end of the 17th century. Ships enter from the Maas River by passing massive gate buildings. They meet busy activity from small craft and big ships in the harbor basins. Many a ship is under construction along the Scheepmakershaven, the basin just north of the Maas. The colorful emblems at the lower rim of the engraving suggest wealth and prosperity, indicating that Rotterdam is a market for products from all over the world.*

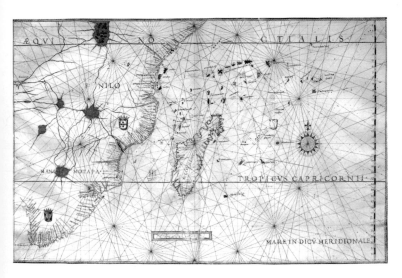

In 1950, the W. A. Englebrecht collection came to the museum, a true enrichment of its treasures. Apart from some fifteen contemporary 17th- and 18th-century ship models, this collection included 280 nautical charts from the 16th to 18th centuries, 150 atlases, and about the same number of manuscript and printed journals concerning the Dutch expansion history of that period. The size and, especially, the quality of the collection lifted the museum's holdings of historical cartographic materials to a top level.

The 19th-century master of the rolls J. C. de Jonge assembled a large collection of drawings, prints, and archival materials dealing with Dutch naval history. When de Jonge's portfolios entered the museum's collection in 1942, they meant a real enrichment of its research and exhibit potential.

A truly outstanding collection is that of twenty-nine models of Dutch wooden and iron sailing vessels for inland navigation from the period 1850 to 1950. The collection is unique for its completeness and for the excellent quality of the models. These were built with meticulous care by father Daniel and son Jelle Hazenberg between 1910 and 1976.

In 1867, the Dutch naval authorities had a turret-ram coastal-defense vessel built at Napier's shipyard in Glasgow, the *Buffel*. It was an experimental ship, being built of iron and having a steam engine and its main armament in a turret. Most of its lifetime the nearly 60-meter-long *Buffel* was a naval barracks ship. In 1974 the city of Rotterdam acquired this industrial-archeological monument just before the naval authorities would have had the ship scrapped. The ship was partially restored to its original shape, showing, for instance,

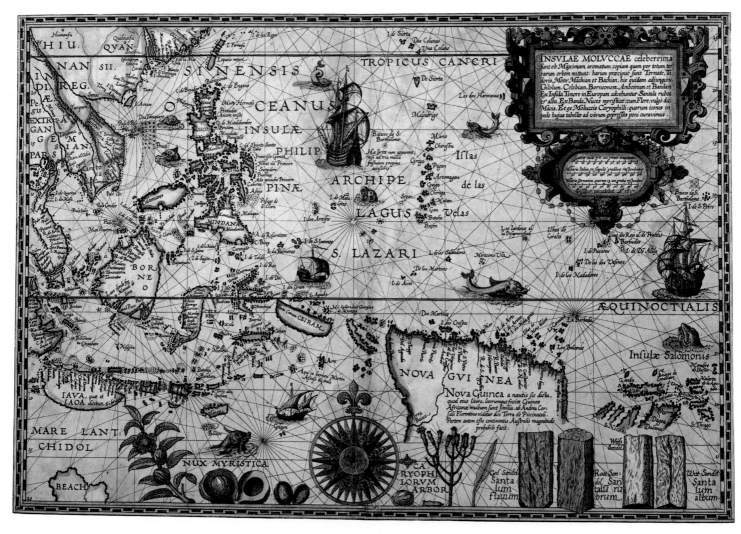

the captain's cabin and the officers' quarters, and was partially organized as an exhibition room to show various aspects of 19th-century naval shipbuilding and shipping. Today, the ship is a popular attraction for museum visitors.

Also popular are two other full-size vessels in the museum's collection: a flat-bottomed river transport and a dugout fish well, both built primarily of oak and dating to the 2nd century A.D. These vessels were found during the excavation of a Roman fortress near the village of Zwammerdam in the province of Zuid-Holland. The fortress was located along the Rhine River, which was, in times past, the northern line of defense of the Roman Empire and the main route for the transport of all kinds of goods and people. Finding ships in such a place was no cause for wonder. The transport vessel measures some twenty-three meters, the other vessel only six. During their excavation, the vessels were taken apart into thousands of pieces, which were then treated with polyethylene glycol to halt their decay. Today, both ships are under reconstruction in a special room in the museum, the restorer doing his job in full view of the museum's visitors and answering their questions.

As is true of any other museum, the greater part of the Prins Hendrik Museum's collections is in storage, a fact that often bothers visitors. To remedy this, the museum has developed a unique system to show interested visitors those items in the collection that are not exhibited. This system has two components: a computerized data retrieval system and a video disc. Although only part of the museum's collections have as yet been made visible on the video disc, the system serves both visitors and the museum staff in a satisfactory way.

With its beautiful collections of models, drawings, and restored vessels, the Prins Hendrik Maritime Museum celebrates and preserves Dutch maritime history.

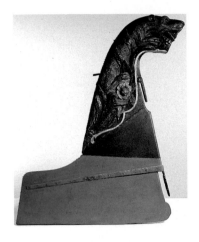

Above: *Rudder of a late-18th century Dutch boyer, a typical Dutch pleasure craft that sailed the lakes and rivers in the Netherlands from the 17th century until today. It belongs to the nobility of Dutch yachts. The completely round hull is characteristic, as are the length-width ratio of 3:1 and the often rich decoration. This beautifully carved rudder comes from an 18th-century Frisian boyer. The otter seems to climb the back side of the rudder in a very natural way, emerging from an abundance of water plants.*

Left: Willem Frederik Hendrik, Prince of Orange *(1820–79)*, oil on canvas by Christoffel Bisschop *(1822–1904)*, signed and dated 1879. The founding father of the Maritiem Museum Prins Hendrik, the prince is portrayed in 1879 wearing the uniform of chairman of the Royal Netherlands Yachtclub with the standard of the yachtclub on his right and the annual report of the maritime museum beneath his left hand.

Opposite: *Secretaire with Japanese lacquer work, ca. 1800, signed Sasaya. This unique and splendid secretaire, decorated with mother-of-pearl and gold by the Japanese artist Sasaya using both European and Japanese motifs, was ordered by an unknown Dutchman to commemorate the battle fought between the English and the Dutch fleets on October 11, 1797, in the North Sea. The upper two oval panels give details about the battle. Beneath them, Sasaya depicts a phase in the sea battle using an engraving by the Dutch artist Reinier Vinkeles. The two lowest panels have a purely Japanese character portraying landscapes from the province of Omi.*

ZEESLAG TUSSCHEN DE
BATAAFSCHE EN ENGELSCHE
VLOOTEN OP DE HOOGTE VAN
EGMOND, DEN 11 OCTOBER
DES IAARS 1797

STVANDE DE BATAAFSCHE
VLOOT ONDER BEVEL VAN
DEN ADMIRAAL DE WINTER
EN DE ENGELSCHE ONDER DEN
ADMIRAAL DUNCAN

NORWAY
THE NORSK SJØFARTSMUSEUM, OSLO

by Bård Kolltveit, Museum Director

Standing on the deck of a ship approaching Oslo, the visitor cannot help but spot a conspicuous, modern, triangular brick building located on the waterfront in a small park at the harbor entrance. The building may remind the visitor of a ship's bow heading out to sea. This building houses the Norsk Sjøfartsmuseum.

The museum was founded in 1914, following a large national exhibition held to commemorate the centenary of the Norwegian Constitution. The maritime pavilion formed a central part of the exhibition, with models, paintings, navigational instruments, and other related materials that had been collected from all over the country. It was a natural consequence to make these articles from Norway's maritime past the nucleus of a Norwegian maritime museum.

For other reasons, too, the time was ripe to start such a museum. Norway's merchant fleet was then completing the transition from sail to steam, a belated change compared to most other European maritime nations. The capability of building, purchasing, and operating sailing ships at competitive freight rates, however, had made Norway one of the world's leading seafaring nations during the 19th century.

Six decades passed from the founding of the museum to the creation of a suitable monument to Norwegian seafaring and seafarers. During those years, there were compromises with rented localities and a half-finished museum building, but the ultimate aim was never out of sight. The building site was secured just before World War II, an architectural contest was arranged in 1953, and, in 1958, the first step in the building process—the Boat Hall—was completed. The central building followed in 1960, with storage spaces, workshop, library, and staff offices, as well as the museum's restaurant Najaden and the magnificent central hall. Finally, in 1974, the main gallery was opened to the public by King Olav V, the museum's high protector. The architects Trond Eliassen and Birger Lambertz-Nilssen won several architectural awards for the building.

Opposite: *Few maritime museums can match the physical setting of the Norsk Sjøfartsmuseum. The three-masted schooner* Svanen *has her regular berth right in front of the exhibition building. (Photo by Terje Olsen)*

Following pages: *The Steamer* Nyland, *gouache by F. M. Sørvig, 1873. Frederik Martin Sørvig, from Bergen, was one of Norway's most highly skilled and prolific painters of ship portraits. This gouache conveys his artistry and correctness in details.*

Next to the Norsk Sjøfartsmuseum are the museums dedicated to Thor Heyerdahl's balsa raft *Kon-Tiki* and papyrus boat *Ra II,* and the polar vessel *Fram*, which carried the expeditions of Fridtjof Nansen, Otto Sverdrup, and Roald Amundsen farther north and farther south than any other expedition had ventured until then. Completing the maritime image of this area are Norway's greatest ancient treasures, the Viking ships, located only a short walking distance away. These four museums together make the Bygdøy peninsula a world attraction for any visitor remotely interested in maritime history.

While the other museums are devoted to special themes, the Norsk Sjøfartsmuseum presents Norway's merchant maritime history and culture in a complete context. The exhibitions are designed to show man's use of the sea through the ages and how its challenges and dangers were overcome. What were the living conditions aboard these ships? How were they navigated? How were they safeguarded from the dangers of the sea?

The collections in the main building emphasize the traditional theme of the development of overseas seafaring through the ages. The historical aspect is particularly evident in the upper gallery, where numerous ship models and ship portraits are on display. The models range from Viking ships and other ancient and medieval Scandinavian craft to ships used in discoveries, colonialism, and naval warfare between the 15th and 18th centuries to

Left: *In 1825, 52 people left Norway for America in the tiny sloop* Restauration. *The crossing lasted three months. During the following century, 800,000 other Norwegians followed across the Atlantic. Reckoned as a percentage of total population among other European countries, only Ireland had a larger emigration to America. (Photo by Bjarne Ims Henriksen)*

the beautiful square-riggers and the emergence of Norway's merchant fleet as one of the world's largest and most modern in the 19th and 20th centuries.

The major theme in the lower gallery is the relationship among man, ship, and sea, with the sense of what a ship is as a means of transport and as a place for working and living conveyed through several restored ship interiors. Visual contact between the past and present is provided by large windows facing Oslo's harbor entrance. Centrally located is an original deckhouse from a mid 19th-century sailing vessel. In these spartan surroundings, six men shared the same space as that available to one seaman a century later. To give a sense of the atmosphere of sea travel at the beginning of our century, a three-deck first-class interior section from a 1914 coastal steamer has been restored. Visitors may enter some of these interiors, an experience that enhances the sense of actually being aboard.

How did a small, sparsely populated country located at the northernmost end of Europe become a prominent seafaring nation? This question is the theme in the Boat Hall, third and largest of the museum's exhibition galleries.

Norway's total land area is modest, but the country's total coastline runs no fewer than 20,000 kilometers. The sea made transport as easy as the mountainous terrain made it difficult. Protected by a continuous chain of large and small islands and virtually free from

Left: *The 1,700-grt steel bark* Skomvær *from 1890 was the largest merchant sailing vessel built in Norway. (Photo by Bjarne Ims Henriksen)*

Below: Sophie Amalie. *Built in Oslo in 1651 for the Danish-Norwegian navy, this ship-of-the-line was among the largest and most lavishly decorated warships of her time. (Photo by Bjarne Ims Henriksen)*

Right: Captain Malmstein's Sailing Ship Register. *Meticulously compiled by the late Captain Petter Malmstein, this 80-volume ledger file contains technical and historical data of most of the world's square-riggers of the 19th and 20th century. (Photo by Bjarne Ims Henriksen)*

ice despite its northern latitude, the fairway along the coast gave Norway its name—Norway means "the Road to the North." Equally important, the coastal waters offered a reliable and constant supply of fish. Thus, boats have played important parts in the history of settlement, sustenance, and social development in Norway.

Traditional features of Norway's maritime history are displayed in the Boat Hall exhibition, including lapstrake "clinker" boatbuilding, a handicraft tradition virtually unbroken in Norway for more than one thousand years. Emphasis is also given to the combination of sailor, fisherman, and farmer, so vital to human existence in the coastal areas of Norway, and to the fundamental changes brought about in fisheries by the replacement of open sailing and rowing boats with decked motor-powered craft.

The unifying elements throughout the exhibition are the boats on display, arranged geographically from south to north. Most conspicuous is the forty-six-foot *Opreisningen*, a fishing boat from northern Norway. The tall, pointed stem, sweeping hull lines, and single square sail readily associate this with a Viking ship. Although smaller in size, the other boats displayed bear similar testimony in design and construction methods to their one-thousand-

Opposite: *A decorated rudder head. This ornament was placed on top of the rudder, adding weight and thus preventing the rudder from getting unhinged. (Photo by Bjarne Ims Henriksen)*

Above: *The Viking longship heritage is evident in the traditional north Norwegian fishing boats called* fembørings. *They have sharp, pointed stems, sweeping hull lines, and a large, single square sail. (Photo by Bjarne Ims Henriksen)*

year-old forebears. Boatbuilding tools, fishing tackle, herring barrels, and racks with dried codfish add visual and odorous effects to this memorial hall to coastal Norway. The Boat Hall also has sections devoted to modern fisheries, yachting, and primitive craft.

The open grounds that surround the museum buildings reflect Norway's maritime heritage as well. An immediate eye-catcher is the museum's largest open-air exhibit, the sloop *Gjøa*, preserved in a dry dock. Commanded by Roald Amundsen, she was the first vessel to conquer the Northwest Passage, in 1903-6. Furthermore, *Gjøa* is a fine example of the Norwegian coastal trader of the 19th century. Nearby stands a memorial in honor of the 4,500 Norwegian sailors who gave their lives to the Allied cause during World War II. A small lighthouse, a storehouse, and a few old boathouses from northern and western Norway are placed along the waterfront, further enhancing the maritime appearance of the area.

Moored in front of the museum is the three-masted fore-and-aft schooner *Svanen,* built in 1916 and owned by Norsk Sjøfartsmuseum since 1973. She combines the functions of a museum ship and a floating activity center for youth clubs and school groups. Laid up during the winter, she does weekly cruises in summer. *Colin Archer* (1893), the first of Norway's gaff-rigged rescue cutters, also belongs to the museum, as does *Venus,* a racing sloop. Both were designed by Norway's best-known boatbuilder, Colin Archer, and both are afloat and operational.

The library of the Norsk Sjøfartsmuseum has some 28,000 volumes of nautical books and periodicals. The ship-plan collection contains the original drawings from some of Norway's foremost yacht builders (such as Colin Archer and Johan Anker), while the photograph archive holds more than 50,000 prints. The written archival material is also quite substantial.

Since the 1950s, the Norsk Sjøfartsmuseum has been actively engaged in excavating wreck sites along the Norwegian coastline. While little usually remains but small fragments of hulls, thousands of various items from these investigations have yielded invaluable information about seaborne trade and daily life in the past, information that would otherwise have been unattainable. Reports on these excavations as well as other maritime-related articles and monographs are regularly published in the museum's yearbook.

The collections and displays of the Norsk Sjøfartsmuseum differ from those of most other countries by the absence of the splendor and heroism so often associated with major sea powers from the 16th to 19th centuries. Here are no grand paintings of battle scenes and very few curious and precious objects from distant colonies. Such items belong to a time when much of Norway's overseas shipping and trade policy was controlled by Copenhagen, since Norway was then united with Denmark.

The uniqueness of Norway's historic conquest of the sea lies on another level: the small, swift, and supple Viking longships; the fishing craft; the blunt, weather-beaten, hog-backed timber barks; and a merchant fleet that grew into one of the largest and most modern in the world in the middle of the 20th century. These aspects of maritime history are fundamental to the presentation policy of the Norsk Sjøfartsmuseum.

Opposite, top: *In 1886, this small gaff-rigged double-ender named* Ocean *sailed across the Atlantic under the command of Captain Magnus Andersen. "Silk picture," probably made in New York immediately after the crossing.*

Opposite, bottom: *Seven years later, Andersen repeated this exploit with the* Viking, *a replica of the Gokstad Viking ship. Hjalmar Johnsen's striking painting commemorates the triumphant arrival at the World's Fair in Chicago in 1893.*

PORTUGAL

THE MUSEU DE MARINHA,

LISBON

·by R. Freire Montez, Administrator, and
J. Martins e Silva, Assistant Director

One cannot write about Lisbon's Museu de Marinha without underlining the importance of the sea in the history and life of Portugal. The nation's location, situated in the extreme southwest of Europe, with the Atlantic and Spain as its frontiers, has made Portugal rely on the sea from the earliest moments of its independence in the 12th century. The sea, in fact, offered the only chances for survival and expansion.

Intense commerce along maritime routes, mainly with northern Europe and the Mediterranean, transformed the Tejo, the river that flows past Lisbon, into a forest of masts and made the city a cosmopolitan center visited by Florentines, Catalans, Germans, Genoese, and Venetians.

At the end of the 15th century, Portugal launched itself on what was, considering the nation's size, an enormous enterprise: her navigators penetrated the unknown and legendary Atlantic, and after they had landed in the Madeira Islands and the Azores, they began to explore down the west coast of Africa. Gil Eannes rounded Cape Bojador in 1434, Nuno Tristão sailed down to Cape Branco (Blanco) in 1441, Diogo Gomes explored the rivers of Guinea in 1456, Diogo Cão entered the Congo River up to Ielala in 1482 and made contact with the king of the Congo. Finally, in 1488, Bartolomeu Dias discovered the route to the southeast around southern Africa and the Cape of Good Hope and landed in the bay of "S. Bras" (Mossel Bay). For the first time, it was understood that India could be reached by going around the coast of Africa and that the Indian Ocean was not an inland sea, as represented in 15th-century versions of Ptolemy's maps.

Vasco da Gama left Lisbon in 1497, arrived at Mombasa in April 1498, and anchored in Calicut on May 20. This was the culmination of a plan of expansion started by Henry the Navigator and supported by the intelligence and diplomacy of King John II. Portuguese expansion did not stop at Africa and India: Pedro Alvares Cabral discovered Brazil and the island of Madagascar in 1500, and the coast of Florida was explored in 1501. D. Lourenco de Almeida reached Ceylon (Sri Lanka) in 1506, Diogo Gomes de Sequeira arrived at Sumatra and Malacca in 1509, discovering the Mascarene Islands in 1511, and Francisco Serrão

Opposite: *Polychromatic wooden sculpture from the 15th century, representing the archangel* St. Rafael. *It accompanied Paulo da Gama, who sailed in the fleet in which Vasco da Gama discovered the route to India in 1497–98. (All photographs in this chapter by Reinaldo de Carvalho)*

Above: *The Museu de Marinha was installed in 1962 in the north and west wings of the monastery of Jerónimos, in the historical area of Belem, in Lisbon. Only about 100 meters away from the site was the beach from which, for many centuries, Portuguese ships left on their voyages of discovery and exploration of continents and oceans.*

Following pages: *Oil painting from the mid 19th century, by an unknown Chinese artist, showing the port of Macao, with a Portuguese gunboat and merchant vessels of various nations. Macao had been under Portuguese administration since 1557, when the mandarin of Canton conceded it to Portugal as a reward for using its ships to eliminate the pirates in the delta of the Canton River. Macao will return to the jurisdiction of the Republic of China in December 1999.*

MACAO

reached the Moluccas and Timor in 1512. Jorge Alvares arrived in China at the mouth of the Canton River in 1513, and João Alvares Fagundes explored the North American coast from Newfoundland to the St. Lawrence River in 1519-20. Finally, the Portuguese reached Japan (Tanegashima Island) in 1543.

By way of this coordinated effort, Portugal was the first modern European power to spread its political, economic, social, and scientific influence beyond its continent, causing what could be called an explosion of the traditional horizons of knowledge. During the 15th and 16th centuries, Portuguese discoveries operated a revolution in learning and culture through the accumulation of new scientific data of planetary interest. This knowledge, gained by experience, had no parallel in the Renaissance world.

This rich harvest of experimental knowledge was spread throughout Europe by the exportation of pilots, navigators, and cartographers. In the 16th century alone, sixty Portuguese were serving in Spain, twenty-five in France, and six in England. At the same time, books on seamanship and geography were printed, filled with information about man and nature in a global vision of the world. The city of Lisbon became a center of technical and scientific developments in the fields of nautical astronomy, cartography, the magnetism of the earth, military construction, hydrography, botany, zoology, geography, and anthropology.

With a past so linked to the sea and nautical science, Portugal's Museu de Marinha reflects the richness of the skills and knowledge that Portuguese navigators were the first to bring to Europe.

The museum itself can be said to have begun with the royal collection formed around the end of the 18th century. This included many models of ships that had to have the king's approval before being built.

In 1863, King Louis I, the only Portuguese monarch to follow a naval career before ascending the throne, officially created the Museu de Marinha, integrating into it the collection of the royal palace of Ajuda. The museum served the Naval College by enabling future officers to gain adequate training from the accurate models.

In 1916, a terrible fire destroyed a considerable number of these models, but since that time, through endowments, acquisitions, and donations, the museum's collection was so enlarged that it was necessary to move it to another site in 1948. These quarters, though larger, were only provisional.

Finally, in 1962, the government decided the museum should be housed permanently in a more appropriate site in the historic monastery of Jerónimos, where today it occupies the west and north wings. This monastery was built in the beginning of the 16th century by order of King Manuel I on the site from which, in 1497, the fleet of Vasco da Gama left to discover the route to India—a feat that caused repercussions that lasted for centuries. At the speed the collection grew, it soon became necessary to expand into a larger area, since the monastery was not large enough. A pavilion was built in 1965 with architecture aesthetically matched to the historical surroundings.

The pavilion houses some of the last examples of regional boats, mostly extinct, as

Above: *Oil painting of King Louis I (1839–89) who, on July 22, 1863, founded the Museu de Marinha. He entered the Naval College when still a prince and commanded various ships during his naval career. In 1861, after the death of his brother Pedro V, he ascended the Portuguese throne. He kept his love of the sea throughout his life. He died in his summer residence in Cascais near Lisbon. In his last hour, he asked that he be moved to a window so that he could see the sea.*

Opposite, top: *Model of a fishing boat called a* muleta, *probably of Mediterranean origin, which was used until the beginning of this century on the Tejo River and at sea not far from Lisbon. It had a curious arrangement of sails that could be trimmed so that the boat could drift sideways while the fishing nets were pulled in.*

Opposite, bottom right: *Model of the St. Gabriel, flagship of the fleet of Vasco da Gama. It was about 25 meters overall, displaced 120 tons, and was crewed by 50 men. At the end of the 15th century, these little ships made voyages to and from India, traveling many thousands of difficult and dangerous miles with an enormous loss of life and property. In the early days of the discoveries, about half the ships and two thirds of the crew that left Portugal perished in the voyages.*

Opposite, bottom left: *Model of a frigate, in bone, from the beginning of the 19th century. It was made on the island of St. Helena by French prisoners who shared Napoleon's captivity.*

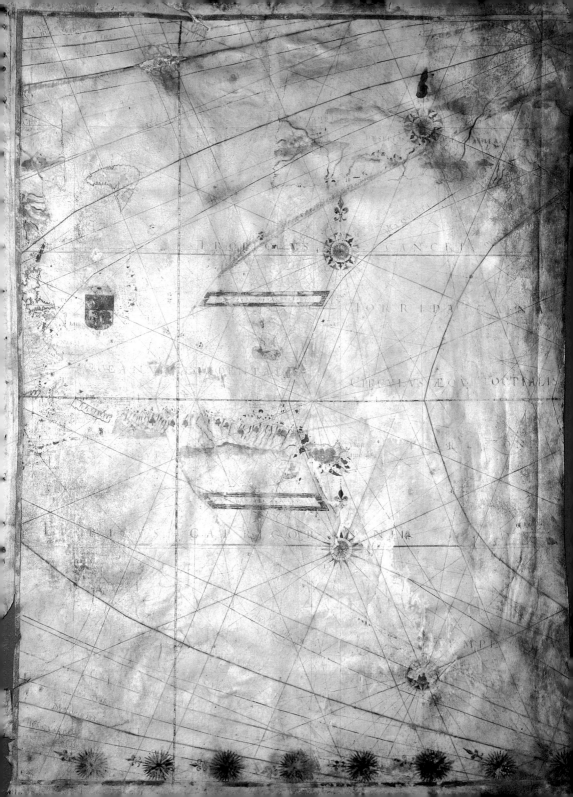

well as a valuable collection of ceremonial barges and galliots from the 18th century.

From a royal collection of warships at the end of the 18th century, the museum has evolved to include all the activities related to the sea, and it now forms a true living record of the Portuguese maritime past. Visitors are offered an opportunity to appreciate the activities of naval, merchant, fishing, and leisure craft of Portugal in the last four centuries.

The great adventure of the discoveries, the golden age of Portuguese navigation, is the basic theme of the permanent exhibition. Most of the objects from that brilliant age have not survived, so only a small number are found in the museum, but they alone are of great value and interest.

There is first a 15th-century painted-wood sculpture representing the Archangel "St. Rafael," patron saint of the ship of the same name, in which Paulo da Gama, brother of the great admiral, accompanied him in the discovery of the route to India. On the return voyage, the *St. Rafael* was lost in the Indian Ocean, but the statue of the archangel was saved and transferred to the flagship, the *St. Gabriel.* Vasco da Gama returned the sculpture to Lisbon.

From then on, for over a century, the image of the archangel accompanied da Gama and his descendants during voyages to India. It was finally left in India and remained there until 1628, when it was returned permanently to Portugal. Since it is the sole object remaining from that great historical feat of exploration, the sculpture is without doubt one of the most significant pieces in the museum.

Two collections of Portuguese artifacts from the age of discovery are considered important because they reveal the technical superiority of Portugal during that period. The first of these is a collection of five nautical astrolabes from the 16th and 17th centuries. These objects, recovered from sunken ships, form the largest collection in the world of this type of instrument.

The adaptation of the planispherical astrolabe to use at sea, the result of work by Portuguese experts, allowed for much greater accuracy in the determination of latitude. The skill of Portuguese navigators was based on their superior technology, as illustrated by the fact that Portuguese nautical astrolabes have been found on ships of different nations, mostly Dutch and Spanish, that sank during the 16th, 17th, and early 18th centuries.

The other important collection is the set of eight bronze cannons from the 16th century retrieved in perfect condition after being submerged in the sea for four hundred years. They belonged to the galleon *Santiago,* which sank in the Indian Ocean in 1585. Portuguese naval artillery of the time was comparatively light, very accurate, and durable. It granted great superiority to the Portuguese in an age when they were competing with the Spanish for domination of the sea.

The most important donation to the museum came in 1948 from Henrique Maufroy de Seixas, a successful businessman with a passion for the sea. Throughout his life he had had hundreds of accurate ship models and boats built for his collection, and most of these are now on public display in the museum. He also collected over 20,000 photographs of warships, fishing boats, and pleasure yachts and recorded with great detail the dates, places, cir-

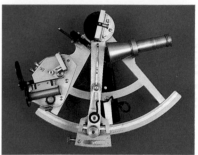

Opposite: *A piece of a Portuguese isogonic chart, ca. 1585, the work of Luis Teixeira, is the first known example of a chart showing the lines of equal magnetic deviation. The chart is of the western Pacific and shows several of the Philippine Islands, some of Japan, and the northern part of New Guinea. To the east are marked, for the first time, the Solomon Islands.*

Top: *Portuguese nautical astrolabe, constructed in 1605. It was recovered in 1985 from the Spanish galleon* Nuestra Señora de Atocha, *which foundered in 1622 off the coast of Florida. The advanced development of Portuguese nautical sciences is indicated by the fact that early 17th-century Portuguese instruments and methods were used aboard ships of other nations up to the end of the 17th century. (This nautical astrolabe is in the National Maritime Museum, Greenwich, United Kingdom.)*

Above: *Sextant, made in England by J. Hughes and fitted with the artificial horizon system invented and mounted by Gago Coutinho. This invention allowed astronomical observations, day and night, to be taken during the 1922 flight by Cabral and Coutinho from Lisbon to Rio de Janeiro.*

Watercolor by Roque Gameiro, painted in the 1930s, showing a 16th-century fleet anchored in the Tejo River, in front of the monastery of Jerónimos, preparing for a voyage to India. Roque Gameiro's in-depth study of the types of ships used in the epoch of discoveries gives his paintings a special degree of technical accuracy.

cumstances, and people shown in the photographs. This enormous quantity of systematically organized and reliable information makes possible the study of various aspects of Portuguese maritime life of the last hundred years. The Seixas Collection also gave the museum's archives hundreds of plans of ships and boats that are now put at the disposal of researchers and modelers.

Among the other collections in the museum, two deserve special mention. One is dedicated to the first flight across the Atlantic in 1922, which was carried out by two Portuguese naval pilots and was a feat that has not been properly recognized, particularly since it took place five years before the famous flight of Charles Lindbergh. The two aviators, Sacadura Cabral and his navigator Gago Coutinho, arrived in Rio de Janeiro from Lisbon after an adventurous crossing of 4,600 miles in five stages, with a total flying time of sixty-two hours. They were forced to ditch their plane twice and were rescued in the most extreme conditions; replacement seaplanes were sent out from Lisbon, and the crossing was finally completed in the *Santa Cruz*, which is now on display in the museum.

Near the seaplane are various objects related to the feat, including one of particular interest: the artificial horizon sextant, an invention of Gago Coutinho that allowed astronomic observations to be taken during the flight by day and night, thus offering very precise aerial navigation, an absolute novelty for its time. Gago Coutinho's invention was later commercialized at an international level and, until the end of World War II, was used by both civil and military aviation all over the world whenever it was necessary to fly long distances over the ocean.

The other collection is of six galliots and state barges, a collection whose only parallel in the world is in Turkey. These elegant and exquisitely decorated vessels were used for many different purposes for about two hundred years. The most impressive is the royal barge, commissioned in 1778 by Queen Maria I for the wedding of her son, later King John VI. The vessel is thirty meters overall and was pulled by seventy-eight oarsmen. It is richly decorated and ornamented with gold-leafed carvings and was used to carry kings and heads of state on their official visits to Portugal. It was last used in 1957, when England's Queen Elizabeth II visited Lisbon. On that occasion, the royal barge conveyed England's queen from the royal yacht *Britannia* to the quay of the majestic Praça do Comercio in the historic center of Lisbon.

The Museu de Marinha is now in a critical period of its existence. As with all museums, it is in constant need of modernization, and like all museums it, too, must face the evolution of museum techniques, making necessary further funding for the construction of new buildings to preserve, in suitable conditions, collections that are now dispersed—in particular those of the regional boats and naval artillery.

The museum also hopes to build a dock at which the existing historical ships and others, which may someday be salvaged, can be exhibited.

Such ambitions illustrate the museum's determination to preserve for future generations the Portuguese cultural heritage linked to the sea.

Opposite, top: *This royal barge was built in the Lisbon Naval Dockyard in 1778 by order of Queen Maria I to be used for the wedding of her son, later King John VI. Intricate gilt carvings adorn the bow, stern, and sides. The stern has a cabin with crystal windows and beautiful paintings. The barge is 30 meters overall and was powered by 78 oarsmen pulling 40 oars. It was used continuously for about 180 years to transport visiting kings and heads of state, such as the emperor of Brazil in 1880, Alfonso XIII of Spain in 1903, President Emille Loubet of France in 1905, Edward VII of England in 1905, Albert of Belgium in 1919, and, for the last voyage, Queen Elizabeth II of England in 1957.*

Above: *The family tree of Henry the Navigator, son of King John and Queen Philipa of Lancaster. Philipa was of English birth, daughter of the duke of Lancaster and granddaughter of Edward III of England. Henry was born in Porto in 1394 and died in Sagres in 1460. The stained-glass window shown in the photograph is in the entrance hall of the museum and was made in 1960.*

Opposite, bottom left: *The Portuguese schooner* Santa Isabel *off Greenland, painted by Roger Chapelet in 1935. This renowned painter, once president of the French Academie de Marine, has many paintings in museums and private collections in Europe, the United States, Canada, and Japan.*

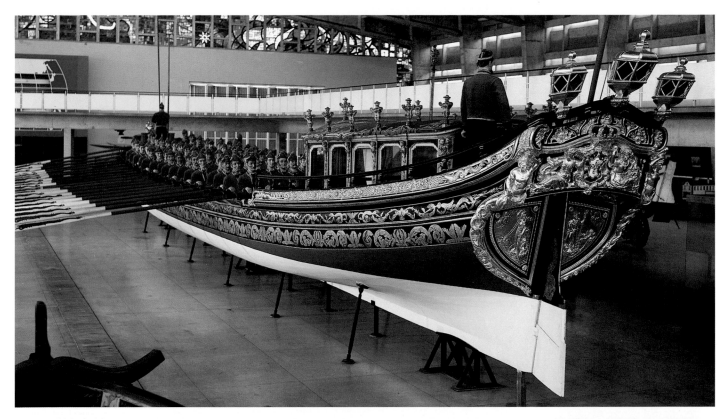

Above: *Swiss pocketwatch with gold-plated case and enameled face and back, made by Bourquin le Jeune, mid 18th century. On both sides it has a circular garland of precious stones. It belonged to the Portuguese admiral Domingos Xavier de Lima, marquis of Nisa, who between 1798 and 1800 commanded a squadron that collaborated with Nelson in the blockade of Malta and was in action in Naples, Trieste, Legborn, and Tripoli.*

THE BARCELONA MARITIME MUSEUM, BARCELONA

by Olga Lopez and Elvira Mata, Curators

The Barcelona Maritime Museum is housed in a building once occupied by the royal boatyards ("Drassanes Reials"). This museum, one of the most important museums dedicated to maritime culture in the Mediterranean area, has had its home here for more than fifty years.

The royal boatyards are in a building that is a unique example of gothic architecture. Located at the end of the Rambla in Barcelona, near the city's port, the boatyards were originally used, of course, for shipbuilding and related activities. Precisely when construction of the boatyards began is not known, but they were first used to provide the monarchs of Catalonia-Aragon with ships and later fulfilled the same function for the Spanish monarchy. The first documentary mention of the dockyards dates back to 1243, when King James I speaks of them with reference to the edge of the Ribera district of the city, where the maritime and mercantile activities of Barcelona took place in the Middle Ages. The later history of this magnificent building includes dark moments, such as the period from the end of the reign of Peter the Great to the end of the 13th century, or the whole of the 17th century, as well as moments of great splendor, particularly during the 14th and 15th centuries, when the kingdom of Catalonia-Aragon was expanding around the Mediterranean and when the shipbuilding industry enjoyed a period of prosperity that lasted until the start of the 17th century. From the 18th century onward, the boatyards were used to carry out military activities not directly connected with the navy, being used first to construct artillery and later, in the mid 19th century, being relegated to the status of artillery depot. This was the state of affairs until 1935, when the army donated this singular building to the city of Barcelona. The Barcelona Maritime Museum was opened a few years later, in 1941.

The origins of the museum's collections go back to the tiny museum of the Mediterranean Nautical Institute, which was set up in 1929 to give some courses for the former Barcelona Sailing School, founded in 1769.

Opposite: *Figurehead "Blanca Aurora" adorned the prow of the corvette* Blanca Aurora, *built in 1848 in Lloret de Mar by Augustí Pujol ("Ferreret"). The sculpture is by Francesc Pasqual ("Ulls menuts") and portrays Maria Parés, daughter of Silvestre Parés, owner of the vessel.*

Above: *A view of one of the four 13th-century towers of the royal boatyards of Barcelona.*

Following pages: *Maritime chart by Gabriel de Vallseca, 1439. It is the most important example of medieval maritime mapmaking in Spain and contains all the characteristic features of the Mallorca Cartographic School, both in terms of the area it shows, the Mediterranean, and in its graphic features.*

Top: *Model of John of Austria's royal galley, made in the workshop of the Barcelona Maritime Museum as a preliminary study for the construction of the full-scale replica built to commemorate the fourth centenary of the 1571 Battle of Lepanto.*

Above: *Model of the submarine* Ictineu I, *designed by Narcís Monturiol in the 19th century.*

Right: *Model of the caravel* Niña, *constructed in the workshop of the Barcelona Maritime Museum. This caravel left the port of Palos with lateen sails, a type of sail used only in the Mediterranean, which were changed in the Canary Islands to adapt the vessel to navigational conditions of the Atlantic.*

This institution accumulated a collection of models and objects related to the sea as well as a specialized library from the sailing schools of some of the towns of the Catalan coast. This was complemented by a number of acquisitions and donations from Catalan ship-owners and other individuals, and the collection was installed first in the new building of the Barcelona Sailing School and later, definitively, in the royal dockyards of Barcelona, where the museum now stands.

Ship models make up the museum's main collection, and there is such a large number of these, of so many different types, that they must be classified into groups.

The shipyard models, constructed in the royal boatyard, are prototypes, actual small-scale models made before the full-scale ships were built. The detail of these models is exceptional, and the precision of their design—they served as experimental models for plans first put down on paper—and the accuracy with which they were constructed give them an intrinsic historical and documentary value that puts them into the category of true works of art. Of all these models, perhaps the most interesting is the 18th-century model of an eighty-gun warship, probably made in Habana around 1740 and then used between 1749 and 1798 as the model for the construction of eight similar warships for the Spanish Royal Navy.

The half-hull models in the museum form one of the most important collections of its type in the world. This type of model shows the fore-and-aft section of the hull. They are usually made in the shipyards where the actual boat is to be built and serve the same purpose as shipyard models. The museum's collection is made up largely of 19th-century Catalan sailing ships built in the shipyards of the coast of Catalonia. These boats played an important role in the economic and human relations between the coast of Spain and the Americas, one of the most glorious periods in the history of the Catalan navy.

The sailing school models were used to teach aspects of navigation, especially maneuvers. The most interesting features of these boats are that they have flat bottoms, although in some examples this was modified later, and that their rigging is technically accurate because these models were used as educational tools.

All the models of this type in the museum originally came from the most prestigious sailing schools of the Catalan coast, nearly all of which were founded in the 18th century as a consequence of the expansion of maritime activity caused by trade with America. From Barcelona, Arenys de Mar, Vilassar de Mar, Mataró, and El Masnou come the most representative sailing boats of the 18th and 19th centuries, both merchant and naval—among them frigates, corvettes, and brigs.

The group of models formed by *ex-votos*—votive offerings given churches in fulfillment of a vow—is small but fascinating. These objects are of great historical value, a demonstration on the one hand of local handicraft and on the other of the religious devotion of seafaring folk. Technically, these are not particularly accurate models, nor do they faithfully reproduce the formal features of full-scale vessels, but they are reminders of a singular aspect of popular culture. The collection of *ex-votos* is complemented by a number of small tables painted as religious offerings, most of which date to the 18th or early 19th century.

Shipping company models were made after construction of the actual, full-scale ship. These replicas were built for publicity purposes, to show the public what the ships were like and to promote the shipping companies. Because of the fidelity of their reproduction, they are of great technical and documentary value. Most of the museum's models of engine-powered ships from the large shipping companies of the 19th and 20th centuries fall into this category.

Another group of models is formed by those constructed in the museum's own work-shops. These are the result of extensive historical research on the part of the museum's tech-nical staff and are of great interest and value because of their technical perfection. Among these models, outstanding are John of Austria's royal galley, the copies of Christopher Columbus's three ships, and the Greek merchant vessel *Kyrenia,* built in the museum work-shop with the collaboration of the Texas Institute of Nautical Archaeology, which is carrying out a study of the wreck of this ship, raised from the waters of the Mediterranean.

The museum's picture gallery contains a notable collection of late 19th- and early 20th-century Catalan works. The finest landscape painters of that time depicted the most var-ied aspects of the Catalan coastline and the towns and villages of the coast. Among these are the works of Eliseu Meifren, Modest Urgell, Francesc Hernández Monjo, Baixeras, and J. Llaveries.

Another interesting section of the picture gallery is that devoted to the watercolours of Josep Pineda. Consisting of some fifty works, these portray a good number of 19th-century Catalan sailing ships and form a valuable and faithful record of the vessels of that time. These works are of the highest technical and documentary importance, as they are in many cases the only records that have survived to the present day.

Also noteworthy are the watercolours of Gabriel Amat, which depict the fishing boats of the Catalan coast, and the collection of engravings made up of works from the 16th to the 19th century.

The museum also has a number of interesting monographic collections. The first of these is the map collection, which includes eleven *portolanos*—harbor guides and coastal charts—drawn by the most important figures of the Mallorca Cartographic School between the 15th and 17th centuries. This school was the driving force behind the mapmaking of the Catalan countries, staying in the forefront even during the movement of renewal resulting from the application of the compass to navigation. Its influence was promoted by the mon-archs of the kingdom of Aragon and Catalonia at the time of their expansion around the whole of the Mediterranean area. Among the items in this collection, perhaps the most important is a *portolano* by the mapmaker Gabriel de Vallseca, dated 1439, one of the most valuable objects in the museum and without doubt the most important item of medieval nautical cartography in Spain.

Another outstanding collection is that of navigational instruments through the ages. This includes a medieval astrolabe from the 15th century, modern gyroscopes, a series of

18th-century gnomons, and a number of 19th-century octants, for the most part made in England.

Of special interest are the 18th-century navigational instruments formerly belonging to the Arenys de Mar Sailing School: pantometers, octants, and Davis quadrants, which are unique in Spain.

The museum's collection of figureheads consists of pieces from 19th-century Catalan sailing ships. All of these, over the long years of their lives, have gone through experiences that threatened their existence and that now form part of their histories. Among these, one of the most interesting is the figurehead known as the "Negre de la Riba," the figure of a

warrior that, when the ship it decorated had been scrapped, stood for many years outside a nautical supply store. Also interesting are the "Ninot," which portrays a sailing school pupil and once decorated the front of a Barcelona tavern, and the "Blanca Aurora," a female figure representing the daughter of the owner of the corvette of the same name, which sailed in the mid 19th century.

An important chapter in the history of the submarine has its place, too, in the museum. This deals with the construction in 1859 of the submarine *Ictineu* by its inventor, Narcís Monturiol, and with the history of this experiment, which although ending in failure was a great step forward in the development of the submarine. Among other objects, the museum has the models of the two submarines actually built, the *Ictineu I* and the *Ictineu II*, the original plans of the latter, and the flag flown by the tugboat that accompanied the former in the tests carried out in the port of Barcelona.

Some of the other collections in the museum contain objects decorated by motifs representing the sea or ships. These include an important collection of 18th- and 19th-century ceramics, boats, and other objects made of silver from different periods, and even items of personal use.

The full-scale boats in the museum are one of its major attractions. The museum owns a valuable collection of fishing boats from all over the Spanish coastline that were used in the fishing industry right up to the time of their acquisition by the museum. Of these, one of the most interesting is the *Jean et Marie,* a boat originally from the Catalan region of the south of France, donated by the Cotlliure Latin Sailing Association. Also worthy of attention are the caro *Papet* and the trawler *Madrona,* both of which were restored by the museum workshop in a successful attempt to preserve the maritime heritage of the Catalan coastline, a heritage in serious danger of being lost. Besides these boats from the Barcelona area, other vessels from more faraway lands are included, among them a Brazilian raft and Guinean canoes.

To commemorate the fourth centenary of the 1571 Battle of Lepanto, in which a Christian fleet, known as the Holy League and commanded by John of Austria, defeated a Turkish fleet (and in which Cervantes was wounded), a full-scale replica of John of Austria's royal galley was constructed at the museum. This boat commanded the ships of the Holy League in the battle and was built at the royal boatyards of Barcelona. The replica, which now has a prominent place in the museum's permanent exhibition, was built entirely within the confines of the royal boatyards, and all the decoration for it was made in the museum workshop.

The permanent exhibits are only part of the museum offerings. They are complemented by a library specializing in maritime history and navigational techniques and science that also contains an important collection of old editions of technical manuals and classics of Catalan maritime history, as well as copies of books that made history in the development of nautical science in Catalonia.

There is also an archive of documents related to different aspects of the nautical his-

Opposite: *Silver ornamental centrepiece symbolizing the discovery of America, by the Munich silversmith T. Heiden. The piece won first prize in the Barcelona Exhibition of Fine Arts and Artistic Industry, in 1896.*

Above: *Cover of the 1592 edition of the* Llibre del Consolat de Mar *("Book of the Consulate of the Sea"), one of the most valuable volumes in the Barcelona Maritime Museum Library.*

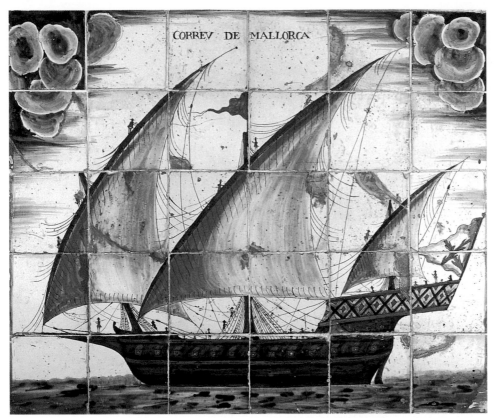

Left: *18th-century Catalan ceramic panel showing a* xebec, *with the inscription* Correu de Mallorca *("Mallorca mail"). This piece comes from the chapel of Sant Telm of the Seamen's Association, Palma de Mallorca.*

Below: *The brig* Francisquita, *watercolour by Josep Pineda, 19th century.*

tory of the country, including trade, health at sea, mapmaking, shipbuilding, and seamen's associations—all of it at the disposition of researchers. A collection of 18,000 photographs documents the history of the Catalan coast, the royal boatyards, and the museum.

In 1985, the museum began to offer a program for schools, "El Museu i l'Escola," to satisfy the demand of that sector of the public, which makes up 30 percent of the total of visitors to the museum. This program includes a series of educational units on various aspects of the museum, guided tours, and a consultation service for teachers.

In 1987, workshops and special programs began to be organized as backup for the museum's temporary exhibitions.

Since 1986, the museum has been immersed in an ambitious restoration plan of the royal boatyards, and at the same time reorganization of the museum itself has begun.

The experiences of similar institutions in America and Europe have served as examples for the museum, which, like them, concentrates its activities on preserving a maritime culture that has played an important role in the history of many peoples. To this end, since 1988, the Barcelona Maritime Museum has conducted a support program for the coastal municipalities of Catalonia that has led to the restoration of boats and other vessels in danger of disappearing. The first step in this campaign was the restoration of a lifeboat in the town of Sant Feliu de Guixols in the province of Girona.

This experience, combined with reflection on the museum's role over the past fifty years and the role it must now play in these times of rapid evolution in both the concept of museums and the idea of culture, led to the decision to carry out an undertaking unique in the entire Mediterranean area.

The Restoration Plan is centered on three basic aspects. First, to make the royal boatyards once more a center of sociocultural activity. Second, reformation of the building and improvement of the area of the city in which the museum stands. These improvements provide the basic infrastructure for the third aspect, the conceptual renewal of the museum. The museum wishes to progress with the creation of a cultural center dedicated to the preservation of the country's maritime heritage.

This preservation will be effected through stimulating greater awareness of the material and intellectual heritage that survives on the coast and is in danger of being lost. This awareness will be created through the conservation, collection, and propagation of the objects and documents that form a testimony of our past and present relationship with the sea—an awareness that will help shape our very identity and that is the basis for our international image.

Top: *Shipyard model of an 18th-century 80-gun ship. This model was probably built around 1740 at the Habana Arsenal in Cuba and was acquired by the Barcelona Maritime Museum from the New Bedford Whaling Museum, where it had arrived after returning to Spain and then passing through France.*

Above: *View of the poop of the 1740 shipyard model. The model was used for the construction of warships for the Spanish Royal Navy.*

SWEDEN

THE NATIONAL MARITIME MUSEUMS, STOCKHOLM

by Lars-Åke Kvarning, Museum Director

T he National Maritime Museums in Stockholm, Sweden, is a state-owned complex composed of two very different museums: the Maritime Museum and the Vasa Museum. The Maritime Museum is a traditional museum with broad collections covering most aspects of civil and naval seafaring; the Vasa Museum is centered around the astonishing find of the *Vasa* warship, which was lost in 1628, raised in 1961, restored, and is now preserved as a stunning museum object.

For the country of Sweden, with its long maritime traditions, it is sometimes embarrassing that the most popular image of the country as a seafaring nation is the bold Viking in his beautiful, swift longboat on plundering expeditions along the coasts of Europe or across Russia to Constantinople. As a matter of fact, the period in Sweden's maritime history occupied by the Vikings has a very limited place in the Maritime Museum.

The quality of maritime museums is often related to the quality and number of original models from different periods. Although perhaps not so very remarkable in terms of numbers, the Maritime Museum's collection of models is of great international interest because they are among the oldest and most valuable that have been preserved. The oldest model in the museum is a church ship from the period around 1600. It is a four-masted galleon with beautifully painted decorations. The ship's origin is unknown, and hence we cannot say if it is representative of Swedish shipbuilding techniques.

During the early 17th century, there was a strong Dutch influence on Swedish shipbuilding. By the middle of the century, King Charles X employed three English shipbuilders: Francis Sheldon, Thomas Day, and Robert Turner. The collection holds several fine models from that period. After this, Sweden's greatest period of model building began. Among those that have survived is a magnificent series of ship models built parallel with the actual ships. After the 18th century, interest in ship models declined and then revived toward the end of the 19th century. Today, although most models are built especially for museum purposes,

Opposite: *Stern of the warship* Vasa, *sunk in 1628. The most decorated part of the ship was the stern castle. On the* Vasa's *stern is the national coat-of-arms. What is now blackened oak was then painted in gold and strong colors. (Photo by Björn Hedin)*

Above: *This 50-cannon man-of-war from the last part of the 17th century is believed to be a ship named* Amarant. *It was a beautiful ship, often used by royalty and important representatives.* Amarant *is a good example of magnificent models that were meant to be showpieces or illustrations for suggested decorations of a ship. (Photo by Björn Hedin)*

The Swedish fleet attacking Fredrikshamn in May, 1790. Oil on canvas from the same period, by J.D. Schoultz. (Photo by Björn Hedin)

other kinds, such as delivery models, sailor's models, and ship-owner's models, examples of which are represented in the museum, are still built.

The Swedish shipbuilder Fredrik Henrik af Chapman (1721-1808) is internationally well known. He was the first shipbuilder to draw and design his ships with mathematical calculations, making it possible for him to foretell a ship's qualities and performance. His *Architectura Navalis Mercatoria,* a collection of 153 ship's drawings and 600 detailed sketches, is an imposing work, later supplemented with a manual, *Treatise on Shipbuilding.* Besides the many beautiful ship models from his time, the museum has in its archives sketches, drawings, and other original documents from Chapman's hand that cover more than seventy years of his production, from his earliest drawing to his last manuscript of 1806. The last ship built on af Chapman's plans was the frigate *Eugenie,* which was constructed in 1846, thirty-eight years after his death.

One of the most spectacular objects in the museum is the stern and main cabin of the royal schooner *Amphion,* famous for having served as a royal residence and chancellery for King Gustav III during Sweden's war with Russia (1788-90). The Swedish victory at Svensksund, south of Finland, is considered one of the most glorious battles of the Swedish navy. The ship itself was notorious for its poor sailing qualities: it was a beautiful ship, but must be considered one of the very few mistakes that Chapman made in construction.

Also from this period is the forecastle from another schooner, *Hoppet,* one of the many sailing ships that carried freight over short distances in the Baltic and North Sea and also made longer voyages, such as to South America and Australia. It offered its sailors poor and uncomfortable lodgings—unhealthy and often infested, dark and crowded. The museum collection permits the visitor to compare this to a ship from a much different period: a cabin for one of the crewmembers aboard a modern supertanker. The living conditions in that cabin are comparable to those of a good modern hotel. The museum visitor can also experience the wardroom from the destroyer *Vidar* and part of the gun deck from a man-of-war dating to the 1850s in which hundreds of sailors slept in hammocks hung between the cannons.

The stern of the *Amphion* is an example of the rich decorations that might adorn the aft part of a ship. The figureheads in front of ships, however, were the most imaginative and, to our modern eyes, the most appealing part of a ship's decoration. There are, as examples, the bold, manly figure from the ship of the line *Dygden* ("The Virtue") and a nameless girl coquettishly lifting her skirt to show her red garter. The museum collection includes many figureheads, both from well-known artists like Johan Törnström, who made most of the figureheads for Chapman's ships, and from unknown artists.

The museum also has a large collection of maritime art, and like all such collections, the artistic value of the works varies enormously. Of primary concern when collecting art for a maritime museum is not how well the work was carried out but what the artist was depicting, be it a ship's portrait, life on board, a harbor scene, or a battle. Of course, such works are quite often fine pieces of art as well. From King Gustav III's Russian war, there is a

beautiful series of small paintings illustrating the course of the war painted by the naval warrant officer Johan D. Schoultz. A later, fine artist was Admiral Jacob Hagg (1839-1931), who not only knew all there was to know about ships but also had brilliant skill at painting water, waves, and air.

THE VASA MUSEUM

On August 10, 1628, a bright and sunny afternoon, the king's new man-of-war *Vasa* set out on her maiden voyage from the Swedish capital. The voyage did not last long. While still in the waters of the harbor, the ship heeled over from a sudden gust of wind, water poured in through the gun ports, and she sank like a stone, "sails and flags flying," as was stated in a contemporary report. The eagerly awaited reinforcement for the fleet was lost.

During subsequent centuries many attempts were made to salvage the vessel, but all were in vain. The most successful such attempt was in 1664-65 by a man named Albrecht

Below: *This table was found in the admiral's cabin in the* Vasa's *stern castle. It has been set with some of the utensils found in the officers' quarters: a bronze brazier to keep the food warm, ceramic and pewter plates, an octagonal glass, and a pewter flask. (Photo by Björn Hedin)*

Opposite: *The* Vasa *was lavishly decorated. Six hundred sculptures and sculpted parts adorned the ship with figures inspired by the Bible and by antique mythology, particularly beings that lived in the sea. This is a caryatid—a mermaid that adorned the* Vasa. *(Photo by Göran Sallstedt)*

von Treileben, who managed to bring up most of the ship's sixty-four bronze cannons using a simple diving bell. This was quite an achievement, as it involved a depth of thirty-two meters. Following this, the ship was more or less forgotten.

Not until 1956, when Anders Franzen managed to locate and identify the *Vasa* after extensive research both in marine histories and on the seabed, did the ship's story again attract attention. Franzen managed to raise interest in salvaging the ship, which was still in very good shape. In 1961, the *Vasa* again saw the light of day and was installed in a temporary museum. Together with the ship came 25,000 other finds, including construction parts and articles that belonged to the ship and her crew.

Hectic work began to preserve and restore the ship. The 333 years spent on the seabed meant that the wood could not be dried without preservation. A new method was developed, using a solution of polyethylene glycol combined with borax to substitute the water, and it was applied to the ship and all the loose wooden parts that came up with her.

The restoration work began at the same time. Those involved faced a giant jigsaw puzzle made up of 12,000 parts that had to be identified and properly located on the ship. Through excellent cooperation between ship's carpenters and museum curators, the restoration work has been carried out—as has the preservation—with good results.

In 1990, a new, permanent museum was built for the ship and has become a new landmark in Sweden. The old, temporary museum had about 575,000 visitors a year, which

Below: *The Vasa Museum, which opened in 1990, is a new fascinating building in the Stockholm cityscape. The building was designed by the architects Göran Månsson and Marianne Dahlback.*

Opposite: *The* Vasa *being lifted to the surface on April 24, 1961—an international sensation. (Photo by Göran Sallstedt)*

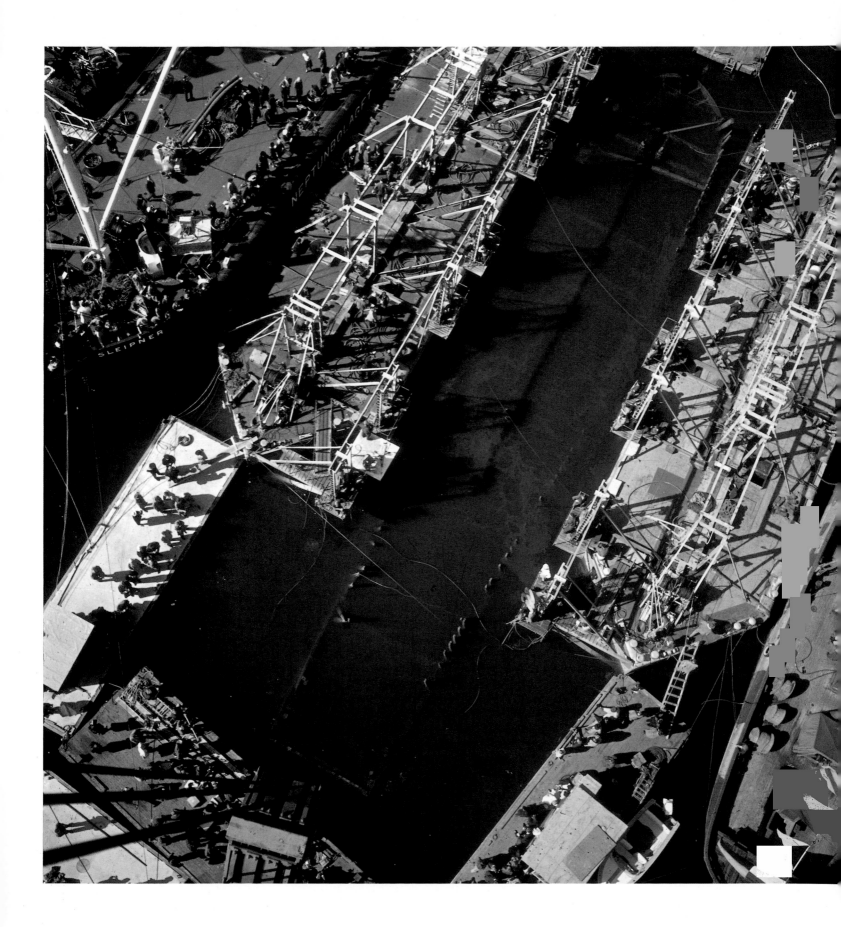

made it the most visited museum in Scandinavia; the new museum is designed to accommodate even greater numbers. The museum has an open design, with the ship as the centerpiece, visible from a distance, to offer a general impression, and visible from up close, to permit study of the details, both in its construction and its sculptural design. The sculptures that adorn the ship are again imposing, for more than six hundred sculptures and sculpted details were found in the mud and clay around the ship on the seabed and inside the ship itself. All of these have been placed in their original locations.

Around the ship are exhibits that place the ship in its context and time and give a glimpse of the society that produced the *Vasa*. There is also the story of its loss, the events around 1628, and its recovery, preservation, and restoration. Since the decorations of the ship are so important, an exhibit has been devoted to the ship and its sculptures from the art historian's point of view as well as from the point of view of the artists working for the shipyard. Yet other exhibits explain shipbuilding during the period and how such ships were sailed and how navigation was performed. Finally, there is an exhibit that deals with all the various sciences involved in the finding and restoration of the ship.

The two museums that make up the National Maritime Museums in Stockholm offer the visitor a broad experience. The Maritime Museum provides a picture of the maritime history of Sweden seen from the widest point of view, from the man-of-war to the pleasure boat, from life in the heat of a steamer's engine room to the elegance of a royal yacht. The Vasa Museum offers the experience of a long-gone past that is unequaled anywhere else, a piece of the early 17th century brought back to us from the depths of the sea.

Opposite: *By December 6, 1988, construction on the new Vasa Museum building had been completed to such a point that the ship could be towed inside it and the wall to the sea closed and construction finished. (Photo by Johan Jonsson)*

Above left: *The 1628 warship* Vasa.

Above, right: *Lower gundeck of the royal warship* Vasa *with wooden gun-carriages in rows along the sides. In all, she had 64 cannons. (Photo by Johan Jonsson)*

THE IRON SCREW STEAMSHIP

THE GREAT BRITAIN, BRISTOL

by Dr. Basil Greenhill, C.B., C.M.G., F.S.A., Chairman,
S. S. Great Britain *Project*

D uring the first half of the 19th century, Britain became the world's first modern industrialized state. Exploiting the natural resources of iron and coal, the nation's industries rapidly developed steam machinery and applied it to every kind of manufacturing. Steam was also adapted to land transport, a railroad system spread over the whole country, and along the railroads a telegraph system grew that was the beginning of modern electronic communications. Britain's manufactures were exported worldwide, almost entirely in sailing ships, but wooden paddle-wheel steamships soon became common on short sea routes to Europe.

The paddle wheel, however, was not an efficient means of propelling an oceangoing ship. Wooden vessels, built from hundreds of pieces of timber fastened with metal spikes or wooden pins, simply could not stand the strains imposed by heavy engines of hundreds of horsepower. By the 1830s it had become obvious that the bigger the ship the more efficient and more profitable she was likely to be.

The solution lay in building big ships of iron propelled by the modern ship's screw propeller. The Great Western Railway Company had built a railroad from London to Bristol on the west coast of England. Their consultant was Isambard Kingdom Brunel, one of history's greatest and most colorful engineers. Legend has it that when the railway was finished he told a board meeting of the company, "Well, gentlemen, you have a railway from London to Bristol! Why not continue it to New York?"

This idea was typical of Brunel's innovative and daring genius. He was a great believer in the importance of the freedom of the entrepreneur, and impatient of government regulation. "No man," he wrote, "however bold or however high he may stand in his profession, can resist the benumbing effect of rules laid down by authority." When he was rebuked by the War Department for placing a contract to build a hospital he had designed to relieve the appalling conditions in which British troops were being nursed during the Cri-

Opposite: *With five of her six masts in place (the jigger cannot be stepped until the engine is rebuilt,)* The Great Britain, *the world's first modern ship, shows herself as beautiful as she is historically important. (Photo from SWPA)*

Following pages: S.S. *Great Britain* Being Warped Out of Avon Dock, *oil on canvas by Joseph Walter, ca. 1845. (Photo from SWPA)*

mean War with Russia of 1854-56 he replied, "Such a course may possibly be unusual in the execution of government work, but it involves only an amount of responsibility which men in my profession are accustomed to take . . ."

The Great Western Steamship Company was formed, and Brunel designed a big four-masted, paddle-driven steamship. Called *The Great Western,* she was the first successful steam-driven transatlantic passenger liner. The company then decided to build a sister ship, another big paddler. But at this time, in the late 1830s, technology was advancing almost as quickly as it is today, and while the ship was in the design stage, iron plates became available at a low enough price and in sufficient quantities to make possible the revolutionary step of building the ship in this material. At the same time the problem of correcting the compass of an iron ship was (as it was thought) solved by the work of George Biddell Airy, the British Astronomer Royal. The Great Western Steamship Company therefore decided to build their new ship of iron.

While the ship was being built, the Ship Propeller Company, formed to promote and market a patent for improved screw propulsion, sent their demonstration ship, the *Archimedes,* to Bristol. After exhaustive tests, Brunel was satisfied that screw propulsion should be adopted in the new ship. Partly built paddle engines were scrapped, and a new power unit was designed that was the most powerful steam engine ever built—it developed 1,000 nominal horsepower—together with the world's first big screw propeller. Numerous technical problems had to be overcome for the first time on this scale, problems of power transmission, of lubrication, of the design of bearings. In many ways, engineering had to be developed to build this great ship.

She was launched as *The Great Britain,* a 3,500-ton, 322-foot-long, fully powered screw steamer with a very sophisticated six-masted schooner rig for "sail assist." She was by

Opposite: *The great A-shaped engine frames, an integral part of the vessel's structure, being installed. (Photo from SWPA)*

Below, left: *In the dock in which she was built, the rebirth of* The Great Britain *begins. (Photo from SWPA)*

Below, right: *The restoration work on the forward part of the vessel's interior structure. (Photo from SWPA)*

Following pages: S.S. *Great Britain* at Sea, *1845, oil on canvas by Keith A. Griffin, ca. 1970. (Copyright S.S. Great Britain Project, 1970/71)*

Left: *A view of the stern of* The Great Britain *before restoration began.*

Below: *On July 5, 1970,* The Great Britain, *afloat on her own bottom again, passed under Brunel's great Suspension Bridge over the Avon Gorge at Bristol. The bridge had not been built yet when she passed downstream after her completion in 1844.*

far the largest ship ever to have been built and remained the largest ship in the world for many years. She was the first modern ship, incorporating in her design many entirely new features that became standard shipbuilding practice to the present day. The beautiful shape of her hull anticipated the American clippers of the 1840s.

The Great Britain went into service as a passenger liner on the New York run. She was just beginning to pay her way when she was run ashore on the Irish coast as a result of gross navigational error. The Great Western Steamship Company went into liquidation, and *The Great Britain* was sold, refitted, and put in the passenger trade to Australia. In this business, she made thirty-two round-trip voyages, interspersed with three voyages to New York and periods as a troopship during the Crimean War in 1855 and the Indian Mutiny in 1857.

She was a highly successful ship, both profitable and very popular with her passengers. During those years she took some 15,000 people to Australia. Many diaries, letters, and

Above: *The beauty of* The Great Britain's *counter stern is now revealed again. (Photo from SWPA)*

other records remain that show how passengers fared, and from these a detailed picture of 19th-century life can be reconstructed.

In 1876, *The Great Britain* could not compete with more modern compound-engine vessels, and she was withdrawn from service. Practically indestructible, she was recommissioned as a sailing vessel, her engines stripped out of her, and put in trade between South Wales and San Francisco, with coal out and wheat home, rounding Cape Horn twice on each voyage. On the third voyage, in 1886, she was damaged by storms off the Horn and put into the Falkland Islands, where her upper masts were sent down, and she became a floating storehouse for wool and coal. Here she lay until 1937, when she was abandoned, partly sunk.

Her fame lived on, and in 1967 Dr. Ewan Corlett, one of today's most distinguished naval architects, wrote to *The Times* in London pointing out that *The Great Britain* was "one of the very few really historic ships still in existence." His letter led to the formation of a group set on salving her. Dr. Corlett headed up the complex operation, found in a personal survey that she was in a condition to be saved, and, with imagination and drive reminiscent of Brunel himself, organized her return to Britain—to the very dock at which she had been built in Bristol.

Today, *The Great Britain* is restored, as far as her external appearance is concerned, to be exactly as she was at her launch in 1844. Because of her role in the development of all modern shipping, she is historically the most important preserved ship in the world. Not only that, she is an astonishing survivor from the early days of the modern world, a monument to the entrepreneurial daring and technological innovation of the greatest days of the Industrial Revolution. It is quite astonishing that she is still with us.

Opposite: *As this nighttime view shows, by 1984 three of* The Great Britain's *six masts had been stepped. (Photo by R.D. Edwardes)*

Above: The Launch of *The Great Britain, lithograph made by Thomas Dunhill, Jr., from a watercolour by Thomas Allom (1804–72). Prince Albert, husband of Queen Victoria, broke a champagne bottle on the ship's stem when the lady who was supposed to launch her missed her aim. (Photo from SWPA)*

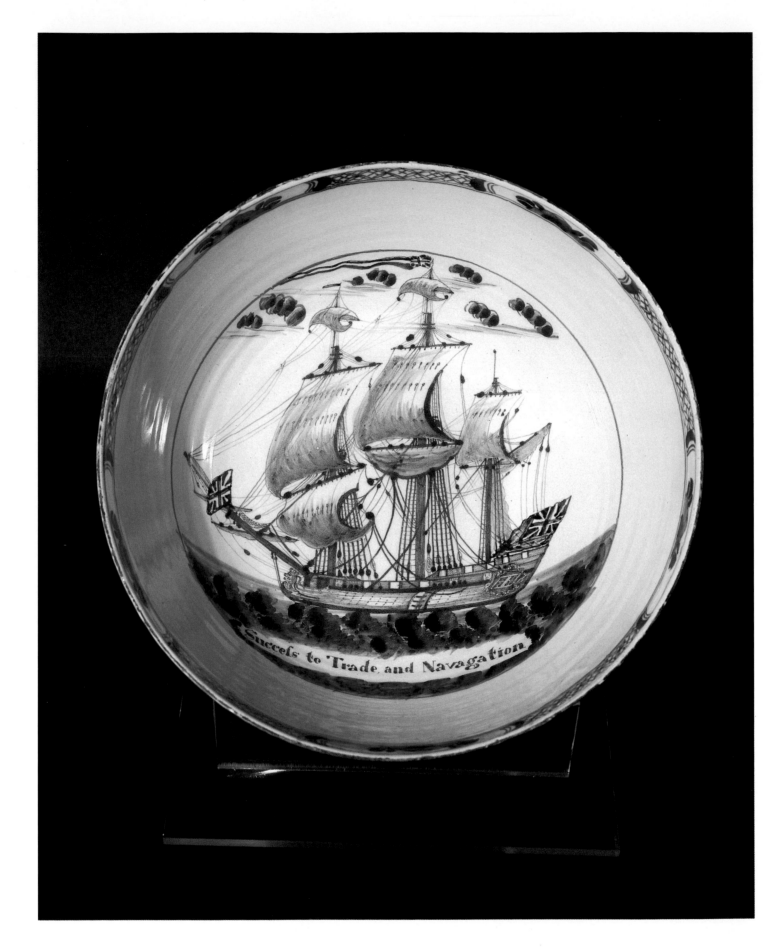

Success to Trade and Navagation.

THE MERSEYSIDE MARITIME MUSEUM, LIVERPOOL

by Anthony Tibbles, Curator of Maritime History

L iverpool lies at the mouth of the Mersey River on the northwest coast of England. Since the late 17th century, it has been one of the major ports of Europe. Merseyside Maritime Museum seeks to reflect the history of this great port and to record the heritage of the men and women who lived and worked with its ships and trades. The collections also illustrate the links Liverpool has had throughout the world.

In the early days, Liverpool's main trading links were with the coastal ports around the Irish Sea, but soon routes were developed across the Atlantic to North America and the Caribbean. Initially, there was one main drawback: Liverpool did not have a large natural harbor, and ships had to anchor in the river. As early as 1699 there were complaints that "it is bad riding afloat before the town by reason of the strong tides that run there." This deficiency encouraged the town council to enclose a small tidal inlet, and in 1715 they opened the first enclosed commercial maritime dock in the world. Over the following two centuries, Liverpool was to build over fifty docks, stretching more than seven miles along the waterfront.

The early growth and prosperity of the port largely depended on a few basic commodities: the export of locally produced salt and coal and the import of sugar, rum, and tobacco. However, Liverpool's name in the 18th century is inextricably linked with the slave trade. It is a matter of record that many thousands of slaves were carried on the infamous Middle Passage from Africa to the New World, but even at its height, no more than 10 percent of Liverpool's ships were involved in the trade.

Liverpool was ideally situated to take advantage of the Industrial Revolution that was taking place in Liverpool's hinterland of northern and central England during the second half of the century. A network of improved roads, rivers, and canals made the port an obvious focus for the trade that Britain's entrepreneurs generated. Manufactured goods were exported abroad, and raw materials were brought in to satisfy the growing industries. In

Opposite: *This Delftware "ship bowl" is one of a large number of such pieces made in Liverpool, which had a flourishing pottery industry in the 18th and early 19th centuries. The origin of these distinctive bowls is not entirely clear. Some may have been made to celebrate the launch of a particular ship. (All photographs in this chapter courtesy of The Board of Trustees of the National Museums and Galleries on Merseyside.)*

Above: *The Piermaster's House was built around 1852. It has been restored to its appearance in the period 1900-20, based on the memories of the children of a former piermaster. The iron swing bridge in the foreground was built to a design of the engineer John Rennie in 18 5.*

Following pages: Bidston Hill and Flagpoles, *by Robert Salmon (1775–ca. 1845).Bidston Hill, on the far side of the Mersey, commanded good views of the approaches to Liverpool. Shipowners' flags were hoisted here when one of their vessels was identified making for the port. Robert Salmon is the best known and most accomplished of the marine artists who worked in Liverpool. He later moved to Boston, where he worked from 1828.*

particular, during the early 19th century Liverpool came to dominate the cotton trade. By 1850, 65 percent of all raw cotton imported into Britain and 80 percent of the finished cotton goods for export passed through the port.

During this period, Liverpool's other great claim to fame was as the major port for emigrants seeking ships to take them to new lives, mainly in the United States, Canada, and Australia. Starting in the 1830s and spurred by the Irish famines and gold rushes of the following two decades, the emigrant trade was an essential feature of the local scene for over a century.

Until the middle years of the 19th century, trade depended on the sailing ship, but steamships increasingly took over on many routes. In 1853, Nathaniel Hawthorne, then American consul in Liverpool, commented on the "great many steamers, plying up and down the river." However, the steamships' huge appetite for coal made them uneconomical on longer voyages, particularly to the Far East. It was a Liverpool man, Alfred Holt, who solved this problem. Originally a railway engineer, he followed his brother Philip into the world of shipping and turned his attention to the marine engine. His invention of the tan-

Below: Liverpool Privateer, *by W. Jackson. During the 18th century, when England was frequently at war with her European neighbours, many merchant ships were licensed to act as privateers. The ventilation ports and impression of a tropical background suggest that this Liverpool merchantman may also have been involved in the African slave trade.*

dem compound steam engine, which produced high-pressure steam from small quantities of coal, gave the steamship the final competitive edge over the sailing ship. In 1865, the Holts founded the Ocean Steamship Company and the famous Blue Funnel Line, nicknamed the Liverpool Navy, which dominated Britain's Far East trade for a century.

The Blue Funnel Line was only one of a large number of Liverpool-based companies that developed a service of cargo and passenger liners running on regular timetables to ports all over the world. As a result, by 1900, one-tenth of the world's shipping tonnage was owned in Liverpool, and it was the largest port for British imports.

During this century, Liverpool has had to face competition from other ports more conveniently situated and offering better and easier facilities. Further, it has had to adapt to tremendous changes caused by the collapse of the passenger trade and the development of huge containerships and tankers in the 1960s. The traditional docks have been all but abandoned and are now the subject of a vast urban redevelopment scheme. At the seaward end of the system, a flourishing container port now efficiently handles record tonnages of cargo with a minimum of labor.

Below: *The clipper ship* Scawfell, *1858, is portrayed off Hong Kong by an unknown Chinese artist. This graceful sailing vessel was built for speed to carry tea from China. In the 1850s and 1860s there was intense competition to make the fastest voyage and gain the best price for cargo. Scawfell's best time was 88 days from Whampoa to Liverpool, one of the fastest on record.*

As befits the port that had the first dock system in the world, Merseyside Maritime Museum lies at the heart of the historic dockland, between the famous Pierhead Buildings and the equally renowned Albert Dock. Indeed, the museum's main displays are housed in one of the dock's magnificent warehouses. Also included within the museum site are a number of historic features and buildings. The two graving, or dry, docks provide homes for the museum's largest vessels, and around the cobbled quaysides are historic artifacts the museum has preserved. The Piermaster's House of 1852 has been carefully restored to its Edwardian appearance and includes a cooperage and a further residence that is now the base for the museum's very active group of Friends. The former Pilotage Building, used by the Liverpool Pilots since 1883, now houses temporary exhibitions but will shortly be developed to tell the wider social history of Liverpool and its people.

Although it opened only in 1980, the museum has large collections built up over more than a century. The largest and most important group of items is the collection of over one thousand ship models. These range in size from miniature models less than an inch long to a twenty-foot builder's model of the *Titanic*. While many of the models are of ships associated with Liverpool, the great value of the collection is its comprehensiveness, with

Left: *The* Marco Polo, *1851, was one of a series of fast sailing ships that carried emigrants from Liverpool to Australia for the famous Black Ball Line. As well as this fine ship model, the museum possesses the diary of William Greenhalgh who travelled on the* Marco Polo. *"Wednesday 4 May 1853 a very heavy gale all night going 16 knots split one of the fare Mainsails. the sea rolling mountains high, shiped several heavy seas. no one allowed on deck heavy rains & great danger out 52 days."*

Left: *This fine figurehead from the sailing ship* Lottie Sleigh, *1852, is a remarkable survival from one of Merseyside's most famous incidents. The vessel was at anchor in the river on January 16, 1864, when fire broke out after a steward upset an oil lamp. The cargo included eleven tons of gunpowder and the ship was ripped apart in an explosion heard 30 miles away. Fortunately, all the crew was taken off in time by a ferry boat.*

Above: *This magnificent centrepiece is part of a silver-gilt service presented to Thomas Henry Ismay, founder of the White Star Line, by the company's shareholders in 1884. A globe of the world is flanked by classical figures associated with the sea and four famous navigators—Jason, Columbus, Da Gama, and Captain Cook. (Photo by Ron Davies)*

Following pages: Loyal Sam, *by Samuel Walters, 1836. This fine atmospheric painting with its strong lighting and exciting portrayal of a tempestuous sea is evidence that Walters was more than a mere ship portraitist. Although an early work, done when he was 25, it shows a sound mastery of technique. His knowledge of ships is demonstrated by the way the sails match the conditions of the sea.*

models from every continent of the world. The variety of models is also interesting, ranging from impressive builder's and exhibition models made by professionals for shipbuilders and owners to naive sailor-made types, more often beguiling for their charm than their accuracy to scale. The museum is also fortunate to have some fine models made by a number of talented and dedicated amateur model makers.

If ships have been an inspiration for the model maker, they have also captured the imagination of the artist. An important collection of oil paintings, watercolors, and prints has been acquired over the years, with a particular emphasis on the ship portraits of local artists.

The artist most fully represented in the collection is Samuel Walters (1811-82), who dominated the local maritime art scene for more than half a century. His maritime connections could not have started earlier—he was born at sea, and his father, Miles (1774-1849), was himself a ship portraitist of some note. The Walters moved to Liverpool in about 1825, and father and son collaborated on a number of canvases. Samuel was a more talented artist than his father and was soon in demand among the local shipowners and masters. His fame spread, and many of his paintings found their way abroad, particularly to America. Samuel possessed considerable business acumen; he not only painted originals in oils but issued many of them as prints. Later, he sold photographic copies of his work and even used small-scale copies as visiting cards.

Other ship portraitists who worked in Liverpool and are featured in the collection are Robert Salmon, Joseph Heard, Duncan MacFarlane, William G. and William H. Yorke, and Parker Greenwood.

A key feature of the museum is the important collection of ships and boats. The largest of these vessels are the Liverpool pilot boat *Edmund Gardner* (1953) and the schooner *De Wadden* (1917), the last sailing ship to trade regularly in and out of the Mersey. Also associated with the museum and moored on its quaysides are the Weaver flat *Wincham* (1948), the Liverpool diesel tug *Brocklebank*, the steam tug *Kerne,* and the Mersey flat *Oakdale*, all run by volunteers. The important collection of wooden boats illustrates the different types of small vessels traditionally found on the Mersey and along the coast and rivers of northwest England. These include fishing boats such as a Morecambe Bay prawner or River Dee salmon boat as well as a number of local types of sailing dingy and gig boats.

The museum is also officially recognized as a major archival repository for documents and records associated with the port. Chief among these collections is the vast archive of the Mersey Docks and Harbour Board, which ran the docks. This includes minute books, reports, and correspondence as well as photographs, plans, and drawings of the docks and buildings, some of artistic interest in their own right. The museum also houses the records of a number of shipping companies and local associations, as well as ship plans and several important collections of photographs.

In comparison with many other museums, Merseyside Maritime Museum is a newcomer, but much has been achieved in a short time. The museum has played a crucial role in the regeneration of the Liverpool docks and waterfront and in the preservation of the city's maritime heritage. As part of National Museums and Galleries on Merseyside, the only national museum in England outside London, the outstanding value of its collections has been officially recognized. In the final decade of the 20th century, Merseyside Maritime Museum intends to build on its success as a dynamic and progressive institution.

Left: *Poster advertising the White Star Line. Between 1830 and 1930, 9 million people emigrated through the port of Liverpool. Many of them were carried in steerage accommodation on board the big liners that ran on the transatlantic passenger service. In particular, White Star liners were heavily involved in the emigrant trade.*

Above: *This authentic reconstruction of the interior of the emigrant packet ship* Shackamaxon, *1851, vividly portrays the conditions emigrants encountered on their journey to a new life. On average, it took four weeks to cross the Atlantic and three to four months to reach Australia.*

UNITED KINGDOM

NATIONAL MARITIME MUSEUM, GREENWICH

by Richard Ormond, Director

ounded just over fifty years ago, the National Maritime Museum at Greenwich illustrates the story of Britain and the sea through the world's largest
and most comprehensive maritime collections. The rise of Britain from an
island on the periphery of Europe to world power in the 18th and 19th centuries was the result of a combination of economic and geographical factors,
but it was underpinned by seapower. Naval strength, combined with an enterprising merchant community, ensured Britain a growing share of world trade by the early 18th century.
Extensive trading activity, and rivalry with other European seagoing nations, led to the
steady acquisition of overseas colonies. Britain's formidable navy was deployed in time of
war on the defence of the nation, protection of trade and empire, and support of land opera-
tions. The navy also led the way in the field of exploration, producing a navigator of genius
in the person of James Cook, whose famous voyages are comprehensively represented at
Greenwich. The recently discovered portrait of Cook by William Hodges, artist of the second voyage, reveals the drive and force of character of this remarkable seaman.

By the early 19th century, Britain was uniquely placed to exploit the advantages of the
Industrial Revolution, becoming the workshop of the world. The country's huge merchant
fleet brought food and raw materials to the home country and carried British products and
manufactured goods all over the globe. In the technology field, Britain was far in advance of
the time and made the transition from sail to steam, from wood to iron, in far greater numbers of ships than the nation's chief competitors. By the late 19th century, over half the
world's tonnage was British, and Pax Britannica was guaranteed by a fleet twice as large as
that of any two major maritime nations. In the 20th century, Britain was overtaken economically by countries with greater natural resources and population reserves. Nevertheless,
Britain's naval strength was to prove of great significance in the strategic battles of the great
wars, and Britain remained a major trading power.

It is this rich and diverse history, extending far beyond the narrow confines of the

Opposite: The English Fleet Fighting
the Spanish Armada of 1588, *by an
unknown artist, ca. 1588. Though
heraldic in treatment, this early picture
gives a good idea of the form of
warship employed by the English and
Spanish fleets at this time, of the stormy
weather encountered by both sides,
and of the skirmishes that
characterized the conflict. In the
foreground, a Spanish galleass,
bearing the standard of the Spanish
commander-in-chief, Medina Sidonia,
is flanked by two English flagships.*

Above: *Lord Nelson's undress coat
worn at the Battle of Trafalgar, 1805.
The bullet hole from the musket ball
which killed Nelson is clearly visible on
the left shoulder. The admiral was a
prominent target for French
sharpshooters, as he insisted on
wearing this uniform. This is one of the
museum's most famous icons and part
of a comprehensive uniform collection.
Trafalgar was the last great battle at
sea of the Napoleonic campaigns.*

The National Maritime Museum, London. A view of the museum looking south, with the Queen's House (ca. 1635) in the centre, flanked by the East and West wings (ca. 1810) linked by colonnades. The Royal Park stretches behind with the Old Royal Observatory (1675) visible beyond the Queen's House.

Left: *Model of the* Minas Gerais, *1908. A detail of the upper works of a battleship of the dreadnought type, commissioned by the Brazilian navy from Armstrong Whitworth of Newcastle. Five hundred feet in length and weighing over 1900 tons, the ship's chief armaments were twelve 12-inch guns.*

Below: *The 1907 steam tugboat* Reliant *is the museum's largest exhibit. It was built by Eltingham and Co. of South Shields for service as a steam tug on the Manchester Ship Canal. Previously called the* Old Trafford, *she was still working in the 1950s, powered by side lever surface condensing disconnecting paddle engines.*

English Channel and the North Sea, that the collections at Greenwich record and exemplify. Set on London's great river, the Thames, artery of trade and commerce, in the heart of dock-lands, Greenwich has held a place in history since Roman times. Henry VIII and Elizabeth I were born here in the great Tudor palace of Placentia. William III and Mary II founded the Royal Hospital for sick and indigent seamen on the site of the palace, now the Royal Naval College, in a superb group of buildings designed by Sir Christopher Wren and Nicholas Hawkesmoor. Behind the college lies the Museum and the Royal Park, and to the side is the famous clipper *Cutty Sark* berthed in dry dock.

The centre of the Museum, and the focal point of Wren's hospital, is the beautiful Queen's House, the first truly classical building in England. Completed in 1635 by Inigo Jones for Charles I's queen, Henrietta Maria, it bridged the main road to link the palace gardens with the park beyond. Recently restored and refurbished, it houses sumptuous sets of royal apartments on the first floor, a sequence of galleries on the ground floor with over two hundred Dutch seascapes, including several masterpieces by the Van de Veldes, who had a studio in the house, and a treasury in the basement.

Flanking the Queen's House and linked to it by colonnades are the East and West wings, which were added in 1810 when the site became a school for the sons and daughters of seamen. The Royal Hospital School moved to Hollbrook in Suffolk in 1934, and the Museum took possession of the buildings and opened to the public in 1937. Several notable

Below, left: *Astronomical compendium by Humphrey Cole, 1569. A virtuoso piece of craftsmanship by one of the great Elizabethan instrument makers, this compendium incorporates in a single case various astronomical instruments, including nocturnal, lunar, and solar dials for telling time, a table of cities with their latitudes, and information for determining high water. It is reputed to have belonged to Sir Francis Drake.*

Below, right: *Captain Cook's sextant, by Ramsden of London, ca. 1770. This sextant was used on Cook's third voyage of discovery to the Pacific and is one of only four known to have survived from his expeditions. It is part of a comprehensive collection of navigational instruments from medieval times to the present day.*

Following pages: The Battle of the Texel, 1673, *oil painting by Willem Van de Velde the Younger (Dutch School). The Anglo-Dutch wars of the mid-17th century are comprehensively chronicled by Van de Velde father and son. This panoramic view shows the opening movements of the last great confrontation between the Dutch and English fleets with de Ruyter's flagship in the centre firing a broadside. The engagement was indecisive. The museum's Dutch seascape collection is the largest in the world.*

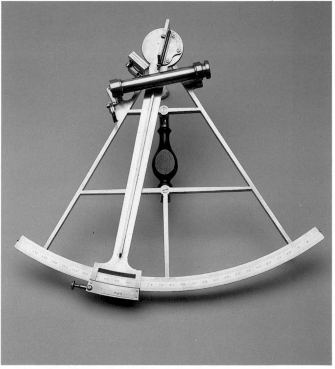

View on Bantam Java from the journal of Edward Barlow. Barlow's description of the voyages he undertook between 1669 and 1703 provides one of the most graphic accounts of early seafaring to survive. The stories of his adventures and privations, illustrated by his precise and naive drawings, make gripping reading.

exhibitions have been held in the East Wing, including Armada (1988), Mutiny on the Bounty (1989), and Captain Cook (1990).

The West Wing houses the main maritime displays. Here will be found the major stories and themes of Britain's maritime past: premedieval boats in the nautical archaeology gallery; seapower and discovery, 1480-1700; the Georgian navy; Captain Cook and the Pacific; the Arctic and Antarctic expeditions of the 19th century; Nelson and the wars with France; Victorian technology; yachting and leisure, and modern seapower. The themes are matched to collections of exceptional depth and quality. The group of Admiralty ship models forms an unbroken sequence from 1650 to 1820 and is unique. It is supplemented by examples of the transition from sail to steam and all the technological innovation of the 19th and 20th centuries. The paintings collection, numbering over 4,000 items, illustrates a wide range of places, personalities, and events. The collections of charts, globes, instruments, ship equipment, engines and weapons, artifacts, relics, flags and uniforms (including the one Nelson was wearing when he was shot at Trafalgar) are similarly comprehensive. Among the largest and most popular exhibits are the *Mary Rose* gun, J. M. W. Turner's painting of Trafalgar, the elegant royal barges, the Tarbet Ness light, and the paddle tug *Reliant*.

Up the hill and separated from the main museum buildings by the Royal Park stands the Old Royal Observatory. Founded in 1675 by Charles II for improving the science of navigation, its earliest building, Flamsteed House, was designed by Sir Christopher Wren. Home of successive Astronomers Royal, the Observatory is famous for its accurate charting of the heavens over the course of three centuries. Visitors come from all over the world to stand astride the meridian line, one foot in the East, one in the West, to enjoy the breathtaking view, and to indulge in the pleasures of the planetarium and the stimulus of the many working telescopes and instruments, including the twenty-eight-inch refractor. Among the most famous timepieces here are the four 18th-century chronometers by John Harrison, which enabled him to solve the problem of keeping accurate time at sea and thus to determine longitude.

The Museum holds over 1 million technical ship plans, 100,000 charts, 50,000 prints and drawings, 750,000 historic photographs, huge repositories of manuscript materials and shipping records, a library of 100,000 books and periodicals, as well as much data on general maritime subjects.

The Museum combines a maritime museum with an exhibition centre, a royal palace, and an observatory; it stands in a royal park and forms part of a famous group of buildings with the Royal Naval College. The Museum has begun to plan an integrated Maritime Information Centre, using the latest information technology, which will provide ready access to the research collections, to documentation on them, and to general sources of information. Offering efficient services to the international maritime community, the Museum will become preeminent in its field.

Below: *The figurehead of the royal yacht* Royal Charlotte, *1824, is an image of the young Queen Charlotte, wife of George III. The yacht was dismantled in 1832, hence the figurehead's unusually good state of preservation. The museum has a large collection of figureheads, including the group from the wrecks of the British coast displayed at Tresco in the Isles of Scilly.*

Opposite, top: *"As Fitted." Detailed plan, dated 1860, of the Cunard Line iron paddle steamship* Persia. *The Persia was the first iron ship in the Cunard fleet and also on the North Atlantic. It is remarkable to view constructional details of such a sophisticated vessel, built only 40 years after iron shipbuilding had been introduced and only 20 years after it had been widely established on the Clyde River. The builders were Robert Napier and Sons of Glasgow and the vessel was completed in 1856 for the North Atlantic service of the company, later known as the Cunard Line. This massive vessel was the first iron ship for the service and was the result of Napier's pioneer work and research in metallurgy. The "chief draughtsman and calculator" of the company, David Kirkaldy, prepared this magnificent ship plan as a matter of love, showing all details, even down to the dial of the engine room clock. The plan is one of the museum's most prized possessions in its collection of over one million plans.*

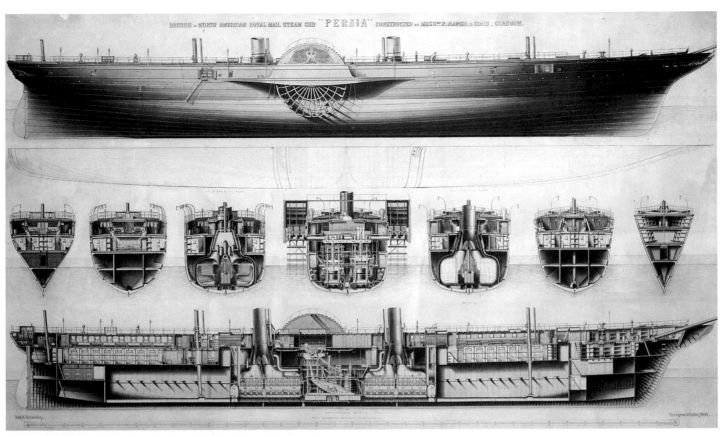

Left: Portrait of Captain James Cook, (1728–79), by William Hodges (British School). Recently discovered in Ireland, this powerful life study is the most convincing likeness we have of the great navigator and explorer. The museum holds almost all the paintings that Hodges carried out for the admiralty on Cook's second world voyage.

Right: The last record of Sir John Franklin's expedition, 1848. This paper, found in a metal canister on King William Island, contains two messages. The first, of May, 1847, reports that all is well. The second records the desertion of the ships, the death of Franklin and of 24 crewmen, and the start of the desperate southward journey that ended in disaster.

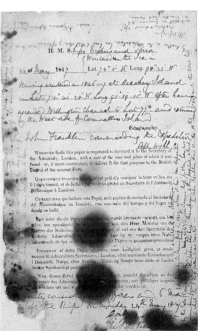

UNITED STATES

THE HAWAII MARITIME

CENTER, HONOLULU, HAWAII

by MacKinnon Simpson, Historian

G eographically the most isolated land area in the world, the Hawaiian Islands have depended on the ocean for their very existence. From the times of Polynesian voyagers, European explorers, and whalers to the international commerce of today, the sea has been the dominant factor in the islands' survival, change, and growth. The ancient Hawaiians husbanded the sea in order to survive. Today, in an uncanny extension of that past dependency, 97 percent of all goods required for modern life enter Hawaii through the bustling seaport of Honolulu. The sea remains the force that most influences Hawaiian life.

The first Hawaiians established a complex, ecologically sophisticated society in the islands, but their isolation was shattered forever in 1778, when two Royal Navy ships under the command of Captain James Cook hove over the horizon. Cook had spent the last decade on three separate voyages of exploration and discovery around the Pacific. He immediately recognized the Hawaiians as Polynesian, writing in his journal that these islands, spread so far across the ocean, comprised "by far, the most extensive nation on earth." As perhaps the greatest Western navigator, James Cook was quick to grasp the noninstrument navigational skills of the Polynesians. Publication of his maps and charts led traders, and ultimately everyone else, to the islands.

In Hawaii, as in perhaps nowhere else in the world, maritime traditions of East (Oceania) and West conjuncted. These two radically different traditions—attitudes toward nature and approaches to naval architecture—are quintessentially represented in the Hawaii Maritime Center's two famous museum ships: the *Falls of Clyde* and the *Hokule'a*.

The *Falls of Clyde* is the last four-masted, full-rigged ship and the last sail-powered oil tanker in the world still afloat. She is on the National Register of Historic Places and was designated a National Historic Landmark in 1989.

Built in 1878 at Port Glasgow, Scotland, she tramped the world for the first twenty years of her existence. In 1898, she was purchased by Captain William Matson to trade pri-

Opposite: *Fresh from drydock in 1987, the restored* Falls of Clyde *is maneuvered through Honolulu Harbor on her way to her permanent berth at the Hawaii Maritime Center on Pier 7. The* Falls *has three historic distinctions: she is the last four-masted, full-rigged ship afloat, as well as the last sailing oil tanker and the only survivor of Matson's original fleet.*

Above: *Dismasted and forlorn, the* Falls of Clyde *is brought back to Honolulu in 1963 after a hasty campaign raised some $38,000 to save her. New iron masts were fabricated locally, and her yards and fittings were donated by Sir William Lithgow of Scotland, whose family shipyard had built the vessel in 1878.*

Following pages: *Hawaii Maritime Center's award-winning Kalakaua Boathouse facility is flanked by the* Falls of Clyde *(left) and the Polynesian voyaging canoe* Hokule'a *(right.)*

marily between San Francisco and Hawaii. In 1906, she was converted to a tanker to ferry 750,000 gallons of oil from California oilfields to the plantations of the islands and then bring back 750,000 gallons of molasses. She later ended up, dismasted, as a floating fuel depot for the fishing fleet off Ketchikan, Alaska. In 1963, she was days away from being sunk as a breakwater off Vancouver, British Columbia, when a campaign to save the *Falls of Clyde* began in Hawaii. Dimes and dollars poured in, and the dilapidated hulk made her final Pacific crossing, this time under tow instead of under sail. In the ensuing quarter century, she has undergone almost constant restoration and the adventure of being almost torn from her moorings in the middle of the night during Hurricane Iwa in 1982. She is berthed at Pier 7, her 260-foot iron hull and four tall masts in stark contrast to the tiny *Hokule'a* moored nearby.

Representing a very different maritime technology, developed over thousands of years, the *Hokule'a* is a performance-accurate replica of a double-hull Polynesian voyaging canoe, and a historic vessel in her own right. Thousands of years ago, canoes like *Hokule'a* crisscrossed the Pacific in man's most epic migration, the peopling of Polynesia, a vast area of ocean with but two units of land for every thousand units of water.

Hokule'a has made three voyages into the Pacific since her first voyage to Tahiti back in 1976. On each of these, the vessel's navigators practiced traditional Polynesian seamanship and guided the canoe using the heavens and seas instead of sextants, chronometers, or compasses. The art of noninstrument navigation, raised to perfection by the Polynesians, ranks as one of the great accomplishments of pretechnological man.

The Hawaii Maritime Center's exhibits are housed in the Kalakaua Boathouse, named after Hawaii's last king, who reigned from 1874 until his death in 1891. King Kalakaua revived a culture bludgeoned by traders, missionaries, and whalers. He was an avid fan and participant in water sports and brought back many Hawaiian traditions, refocusing attention on the Hawaiians' strong link to the ocean. Kalakaua's own Boathouse, from which the museum facility takes its architectural and spiritual theme, was located just blocks away from the site of the new museum building. The Center is scrupulously bicultural, placing equal weight on the traditions and achievements of Eastern and Western cultures.

Located next to Aloha Tower, on Honolulu Harbor's historic Steamship Pier, the museum houses exhibits covering the rich and unique maritime history of Hawaii. A tribute to King Kalakaua and the story of royal regattas at Honolulu Harbor greets the visitor. Other exhibits include Polynesian voyaging, the sandalwood trade, surfing, wind surfing, tattooing, whaling, seaplanes, traditional Hawaiian fishing and canoe making, shipwrecks, tidal waves, sharks, the Matson Line, maritime art, and much more. Many of the exhibits are enhanced by laser disc and audiovisual presentations, including a narrated stereo tape tour of the Kalakaua Boathouse exhibit by William Conrad.

A few miles around the coast, perched on a cliff some five hundred feet above the Pacific, historic Makapu'u Lighthouse features the largest hyper-radiant Fresnel lens still in operation anywhere in the country. Under a licensing agreement with the U.S. Coast Guard, the Hawaii Maritime Center operates educational and recreational tours to the facility.

From voyaging canoes to tall ships and lighthouses, the Hawaii Maritime Center tells the unique and rich history of the archipelago that Mark Twain called "The loveliest fleet of islands anchored in any ocean."

Hokule'a *under sail.*
Her two-and-a-half-year
Voyage of Rediscovery
around the islands of the
Pacific used crewmem-
bers from many islands.
She is currently training
crews for a voyage to the
1992 Pacific Arts Festival
in Rarotonga.

Above: *Makapu'u Light has been a beacon to mariners since 1909. It was moved up the priority list when the Pacific Mail Steamer S.S. Manchuria made a ten-mile navigational error and went aground on the reef in the background in 1906. She was finally pried free, but the need for a light on the headland was established, after almost three decades of haggling.*

Opposite: *Five-time Triple Crown of Surfing Champion Derek Ho riding a tube on the North Shore of Oahu. The sport of surfing was created by Hawaiians, and the first image of a surfboard rider was a drawing by John Webber, Captain Cook's voyage artist, in 1779.*

Opposite: *Matson's liner* Mariposa *docked in Honolulu Harbor in the 1930s. The arrival of a Matson ship was the occasion for a celebration called Boat Day, with music, lei sellers on the pier, boys diving for thrown coins, and colorful streamers in the air. This was the heyday of Matson's passenger service, which was eventually supplanted by airplanes and finally ceased in 1972. For over a century, Matson Navigation has brought cargo to and from the islands and still supplies some 70 percent of goods used in Hawaii.*

Left: *The interior of the Kalakaua Boathouse. In the foreground is part of a double-hulled* koa *canoe display case housing traditional Hawaiian fishing tools. A very rare humpback whale skeleton will soon be suspended overhead.*

UNITED STATES

THE MARINERS' MUSEUM, NEWPORT NEWS, VIRGINIA

by Richard C. Malley, Curator

When the noted scholar and philanthropist Archer M. Huntington founded The Mariners' Museum in 1930, he was keenly aware of the influence that the sea has exerted on human cultures around the world and through the ages. This new museum was charged with collecting, preserving, and interpreting the material objects and cultural traditions that reflect the water's impact on mankind. Though located along the shore of one of America's great marine estuaries—Chesapeake Bay—The Mariners' Museum staff has ranged far and wide in search of artifacts and knowledge that chronicle this relationship with the sea.

Man's seafaring tradition can be measured in millennia as much as in leagues and miles, for nautical archaeology has revealed traces of once-great maritime empires like those of Phoenicia, Greece, and Rome. Evidence in the form of coins, amphorae, even the remains of vessels themselves, testify to the scope of this activity. One of the most striking illustrations of this long maritime tradition is the August F. Crabtree Collection, comprising sixteen intricately constructed and decorated ship models. Ranging from the primitive dugout and raft to the pioneering ocean steamship *Britannia* of 1840, the Crabtree models provide a fascinating chronology in miniature of man's continuing efforts to utilize the water.

.The movement of people and goods on the water highways of the globe has played a fundamental role in shaping our world today. Hundreds of ship models in the museum's collection, ranging from canoes to containerships, luggers to liquefied-gas carriers, show the great diversity of form and function evolved by the world's seafarers over time.

In constructing his vessels, man has often included some form of painted or carved decoration. Just as oculi (eyes) were applied to the bows of vessels in ancient Mediterranean and Eastern cultures, so too were carved symbolic figures found on Western vessels, from Norse longships to steamers of the early 20th century. Human forms abounded among these figureheads, providing the vessel with a sense of identity. Yet other forms, including ani-

Opposite: *This figurehead once graced the bow of the British full-rigged iron ship* Benmore, *built in 1870. The patriotic color scheme was applied after the vessel was acquired by an American firm in 1920.*

Above: *Twenty-six feet of gleaming mahogany, the 1923 Chris-Craft runabout* Miss Belle Isle *retains her original Curtis aircraft engine. The water's role in recreational activities of all kinds is a subject of increasing interest and research. (Photo by Richard Gary)*

Following pages: *Built in Maryland in 1773, the ship* Aston Hall *is typical of many vessels designed for Britain's colonial tobacco trade. Francis Hollman's 1777 portrait incorporates two views of the ship*

mals, were used to symbolize attributes like speed, grace, or power. The magnificent eagle figurehead from the steam frigate U.S.S. *Lancaster* is a prime example. Carved in 1880-81, its eighteen-foot wingspan symbolized the power of both ship and nation. Weighing more than one and one-half tons, this splendid carving was rescued in the 1930s from a Boston ship chandlery by the museum staff. Now part of the largest figurehead collection in North America, this glorious symbol of maritime achievement is the first artifact that visitors encounter as they enter The Mariners' Museum.

While two-dimensional representations of vessels also can be traced back to ancient cultures like Egypt and Greece, it was in Western Europe that seascapes and ship portraitures became specialized art forms. Wildly atmospheric treatments of sea and sky by Dutch and Flemish painters in the 1600s evolved into a more documentary style like that in the portrait of the English colonial tobacco ship *Aston Hall*. Such expressions used a variety of mediums. The crisp image of the American ship *Orozimbo* appeared not only in a watercolor painting but also on the front of a large Liverpool jug.

Below: *Detail of arist-carver August F. Crabtree's model of a late 17th-century French galley showing the elaborate carving found on some of the vessels of King Louis XIV of France.*

Opposite: *August F. Crabtree's model of the late 17th-century French galley shows a vessel whose roots can be traced back more than two thousand years. The Sun King maintained a number of galleys in the early 1700s.*

For other artists, the interaction between sea and land prompted an emotional response quite different from that of the ship portraitist. Such elements as light and water take on symbolic meanings in the work of 19th-century painters like William Bradford or Fitz Hugh Lane. Though Lane's legs were crippled by polio, his eyes and hands were able to capture both the timeless natural beauty of the New England coast and the sense of impending change to its maritime character.

Works from the hands of the mariners themselves are likewise valuable in understanding the sea experience. Journals from the museum's extensive manuscript collection provide intimate glimpses of shipboard life, as do occasional drawings and sketches from the hands of the sailor. Examples of handiwork like the sailor's knotwork or the whaleman's scrimshaw also tell part of the story of life at sea.

The hazards of seafaring have been shared by mariners of many nations and in all times. Safety on the water has always depended on constant vigilance and a respect for the

Below: *Noted carver John H. Bellamy (1824-1914) produced this stunning figurehead for the USS* Lancaster. *With its 18-foot wingspan, this eagle figurehead symbolized the power of the United States. After decades of service, the carving ended up in a Boston ship chandlery, where it was acquired by the museum. (Photo by Gregg Vicick)*

Opposite: *The* Orozimbo *jug of ca. 1805 portrays the Virginia-built ship in a stylized, hand-painted representation. Liverpool potters specialized in the production of these earthenware jugs, which could be decorated to satisfy any shipowner or captain. In the 19th century, various other mediums, such as snuffboxes and ceramic plates incorporated decorative ship images. This Liverpool jug of the* Orozimbo *is an unusually fine example of this genre.*

OROZIMBO, OF BALTIMORE.

forces of nature. Yet even the most advanced technology has not guaranteed man's safety. An unwritten rule of the sea is that mariners help one another in time of distress. Supplementing this code has been the work of private and governmental lifesaving agencies. The museum's collection includes fine examples of lifesaving craft and equipment reflecting nearly a century and a half of continuous development in this field.

The art of navigation also has been a basic element of safety on the sea. Over the centuries, hand-held instruments like the compass and the octant were devised to help sailors find their way. Other types of aids were fixed in one place, to be used as reference points. Primary among these signposts of the sea are buoys and lighthouses, which can mark safe harbors or warn of unseen hazards. An example of the largest class of lighthouse beacon is the first-order Fresnel lens from Cape Charles Lighthouse, at the entrance to Chesapeake Bay. From 1895 to 1963, this multi-ton glass-and-bronze gem, projecting its light twenty miles to sea, guided vessels into the Bay. Today its distinctive light signal marks the entrance to the museum's Chesapeake Bay Gallery.

The Mariners' Museum has drawn much inspiration from its location on Hampton Roads, near the mouth of Chesapeake Bay. The Chesapeake Bay Gallery allows visitors to savor the complex natural and human forces that have shaped the maritime heritage of this region for some four centuries. Themes like shipbuilding and waterborne commerce illustrate how technology has transformed the Bay. A prime example is the introduction of steam propulsion, which prompted great changes by freeing the mariner from total dependence on wind and tide. Symbolic of this change is an operating steam engine from a Chesapeake Bay tugboat, twelve tons of iron and brass balanced like a fine watch. Rescued from the wrecker's torch, today it delights visitors while reminding them of technology's profound effects on the seafarer.

Control of the sea has been a major factor in the rise and fall of nations and empires. As long as merchant vessels have plied the sea routes of the globe, there has been the need to protect them from threats like pirates or hostile powers. Naval forces, developed in response to such threats, have become a common fixture on the oceans of the world. An extensive gallery devoted to the rise of western seapower emphasizes the role that technology has played in projecting man's power on, above, and below the surface of the sea.

Over the last century or more, the sea has become something more than a highway of commerce, or a battleground, or a provider of food. It has also become a valuable source of recreation. The museum's vast small boat collection includes superb examples of leisure watercraft, variously propelled by muscle, wind, or engine. A 1923 Chris-Craft runabout, *Miss Belle Isle*, now restored to original condition, is among the most striking examples of such recreational craft in the collection.

Through the use of artifacts, still and moving images, printed and manuscript material, and live demonstrations, The Mariners' Museum continues to serve the purpose for which it was created—to forge a better understanding of the countless ways in which the waters of the planet have shaped our past and continue to influence our present world.

Opposite, top: *The work of James Bard (1815–97) has proved invaluable in documenting the appearance of hundreds of river and coastal vessels like the 1852 Hudson River towboat* America. *Bard's undeniable draftsmanship, coupled with a wondrous sense of immediacy and detail, lends his portraits a special exuberance.*

Opposite, below: *A classic example of form following function, the Norwegian tanker* Hilli *is designed to carry liquified natural gas (LNG). This 1:250 scale model clearly shows the large storage tanks characteristic of LNG carriers. (Photo by Gregg Vicik)*

L. Brainard, Commander

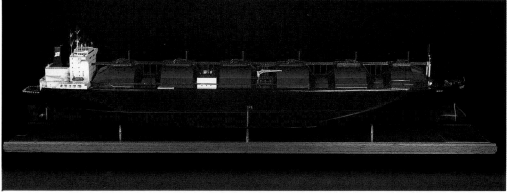

Left: *A superb example of the whaleman's art of scrimshaw, this watch holder was fashioned by Charles B. Tobey during a whaling voyage in 1819.*

Opposite: *Constructed in Paris in 1894, the first-order Fresnel lens from the Cape Charles Lighthouse guided mariners into Chesapeake Bay for nearly seventy years. It now marks the entrance to the Museum's Chesapeake Bay Gallery. (Photo by Gregg Vicik)*

THE MYSTIC SEAPORT

MUSEUM, MYSTIC,

CONNECTICUT

by J. Revell Carr, President

O n the southern coast of New England in the northeastern region of the United States is Mystic Seaport, a maritime museum of unusual dimension. Since its founding in 1929, it has evolved into a complex institution that collects, preserves, and educates with an extraordinary range of activities. While the preservation of the museum collections is at the core of the work of this institution, the focus is strongly on the learning that can be achieved through those objects.

The community of Mystic, Connecticut, created a fruitful, nurturing environment for this museum, which was first known as The Marine Historical Association. With Mystic being a notable shipbuilding center in the 19th century, it was a natural site to gather artifacts relating to the maritime history of the New England region. Mystic Seaport has developed strong collections in the maritime arts—paintings, figureheads, scrimshaw, models—and equally strong collections of the artifacts used in maritime enterprise and recreation—tools, navigational instruments, clothing—as well as exceptional collections of items documenting the maritime story—logs, plans, and photographs. However, ships and boats are the ultimate maritime artifacts since they are the literal and figurative vehicles of maritime endeavor, and Mystic Seaport has become a sanctuary for endangered historic vessels. It is also a sanctuary for endangered shoreside structures, and through these vessels and buildings, visitors experience maritime history and Mystic achieves its distinctive character.

Its site on the Mystic River was ideal for the creation of an open-air museum with historic ships on the waterfront and an assemblage of maritime-related buildings that create the sense of a 19th-century New England coastal community. Maritime scholar Carl C. Cutter was one of the three founders of the museum, and he provided the programmatic vision in the early decades. Through his instigation, Mystic Seaport departed from the course of the traditional maritime museum by acquiring actual vessels. In 1931, the dramatic and elegant sandbagger sloop *Annie,* built in 1880, was acquired. As the first boat in the museum's collection,

Opposite: *Historic buildings and craft shops line the Seaport waterfront, as the sloop* Emma C. Berry *lies alongside the wharf. (Photo by Claire White-Peterson)*

it established a collecting direction that would, by the beginning of the 1990s, result in a watercraft collection of over 400 vessels. It is probably this collection, and particularly the major vessels within it, for which Mystic Seaport is best known.

The young museum had the courage to take responsibility for the last American whaleship, the *Charles W. Morgan*, which was one hundred years old and battered when it arrived at the museum in 1941. The New England region had developed a whaling industry that led the world in the 19th century. There had been more than seven hundred whaleships sailing out of New England, but by 1912 only a few remained, and it was then that an artist, Harry Neyland, launched an effort to save one of these ships. The *Morgan* survives today through the efforts of Neyland and virtually thousands of people associated with Mystic over the last fifty years, who have contributed their skills, effort, or resources to its preservation.

Other major ships include the classic Gloucester fishing schooner *L. A. Dunton*, which was built in the famed Story Yard in 1921 and came to Mystic Seaport in 1963, and the *Joseph Conrad*. Built in 1882 as the Danish training ship *Georg Stage*, the ship's name was changed to *Joseph Conrad* by Alan Villiers when he acquired her in 1934 for a round-the-world voyage. She eventually became the property of the U. S. government and was given to Mystic Seaport by an act of Congress in 1947. Today, the *Conrad* serves the dual roles of berthing vessel for youngsters involved in the museum's education programs and a primary exhibit for museum visitors. The museum's waterfront exhibits a number of other significant regional vessels, such as the Noank wet-well smack *Emma C. Berry* (1866), the oyster sloop *Nellie* (1890), the Friendship sloop *Estella A.* (1904), and the operating, coal-fired steam passenger ferry *Sabino* (1908). Other smaller craft are exhibited afloat, in two boat halls ashore, or in a museum storage facility adjacent to the seventeen-acre exhibit area.

This collection of vessels creates an exceptional document on the working and recreational watercraft of the northeastern United States. The collection is cared for by a specialized curatorial staff in the fully equipped, preservation shipyard.

Originally conceived as "backdrops for the ships," the collection of historic buildings at Mystic Seaport quickly took on its own importance and distinction. The museum was established on the site of the George Greenman & Company Shipyard, where in the 19th century more than one hundred vessels, including the brilliant clipper *David Crockett*, were built and launched. As the museum evolved, maritime-related buildings from locations throughout New England were moved to the museum site. In many instances, the buildings were threatened or endangered. One of the first to be brought in was the James D. Driggs Shipsmith Shop, which had been moved from its original site in New Bedford, Massachusetts, to another location prior to its arrival in Mystic in 1944. Its rescue from neglect gave the building a new life and gave visitors an opportunity to experience a simple metal-working shop that had served the whaling industry. In another instance of the rescue of an endangered building, a 260-foot-long section of the Plymouth Cordage Company Ropewalk was saved and erected at Mystic Seaport. The building was 123 years old when the company ceased using it in 1947. It was scheduled for destruction when Carl Cutter organized an

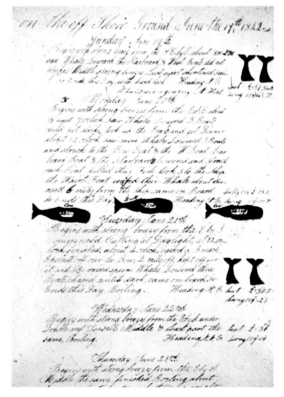

Above: *Mystic in 1869, with the ship* Frolic, *and the hulls of fourteen gunboats that were being built for the government of Spain.*

Left: *The Mallory-owned, Mystic-built sloop* Haswell *is depicted rounding Southwest Spit, off Staten Island in New York Harbor, in this oil painting by James F. Butterworth. The* Haswell *went on to win the 1858 race, and the museum also has the trophy it won in this race. (Photo by K. Mahler)*

Following pages: *The 1888 four-masted coasting schooner* W. Wallace Ward *is portrayed by S.F.M. Badger in this 1897 oil painting.*

effort that resulted in the preservation of a significant portion of the original structure.

Although not on the verge of destruction, the integrity of the 1874 United States Life Saving Service Station at New Shoreham on Block Island was threatened. It was to be adapted for use as a club with drastic alterations. A substitute structure was built at the museum, and when the original station arrived at Mystic by barge, the new building took its place on the barge and was delivered to Block Island.

To date more than one dozen significant buildings have been brought to the museum to join eight historic structures from the Greenman & Company shipbuilding era. Those buildings, along with others that were adapted for museum use or newly constructed, create the environment of 19th-century maritime New England. These ships, homes, shops, stores, chapels, and businesses are furnished and equipped with decorative arts, tools, merchandise, textiles, and manufacturing materials appropriate to each location. In many of these exhibits, expert staff members assist visitors by demonstrating a process or explaining a building's function. Within this atmosphere the museum visitor easily steps back in time and absorbs the history of life at sea and ashore in this era.

While the "living museum" gives Mystic Seaport its special character, the museum has broad and rich collections of the maritime arts and artifacts that are more traditionally found in maritime museums. Mystic Seaport Museum's outstanding collection of paintings and prints is particularly reflective of this region. The prints capture both scenes of life ashore and the vessels that worked this coast or made passages between New England and international ports.

Despite the strength of the print collection, it is the painting collection with its primary emphasis on ship portraits that most vividly depicts the sailing ships, steamers, working craft, and yachts of 19th-century New England. Ship portraitists working in America, such as Buttersworth, Badger, Wales, Stubbs, Jacobsen, Hansen, Huge, Baker, Drew, Bradford, J. E. C. Peterson, and Bard, are all well represented, as are well-known artists from around the world who portrayed American ships. The artists of the Mediterranean, such as the Roux Family, both Cammillieris, DeSimone, and Pellegrin, are strongly present, as are others from Great Britain, Scandinavia, or other European areas. Prolific Chinese ship portraitists created many of the images in the museum's painting collection.

The great majority of these paintings have been donated by shipping and yachting families who have been associated with the museum over the years. Leading among these has been the shipbuilding, ship-owning, and ship-brokering family of the Mallorys. The family began its maritime involvement in Mystic in 1814, and they are still involved today. One of the earliest members of the museum was Clifford D. Mallory, who served as museum president in the late 1930s and whose brother P. R. Mallory succeeded him as president and led the board of trustees for two decades. Today, Clifford D. Mallory, Jr., continues to serve after more than fifty years as a trustee. Numerous paintings of Mallory-owned ships have been donated to the museum, and they cover a range of artists from Jacob Peterson to the Rouxs and Antonio Jacobsen.

As the age of commercial sail faded, so did the tradition of ship portrait painting. However, photographic technology was improving, and remarkable photographic records of maritime activities began to develop. Mystic has an exceptional photographic collection, including the famed Rosenfeld Collection, which has over 1 million images covering American maritime subjects from the 1880s to the present.

During the 20th century, American involvement with the sea has turned increasingly toward yachting and recreational boating. The Rosenfeld Collection reflects this change, as does another remarkable resource, the museum's ship plans collection. While earlier ship designs are preserved in the more than 800 half models in the museum collection, the somewhat later designs were captured in drawn plans. This rapidly growing area of collection has more than 60,000 sheets of plans and is adding the work of commercial and yacht designers, such as Philip L. Rhodes and Sparkman and Stephens. This same growth pattern is also evident in the museum's exceptional motion picture film and videotape collection, which currently contains over 850,000 feet of film and 700 rolls of videotape.

Among three-dimensional objects, Mystic is particularly strong in figureheads, models, scrimshaw, and navigational instruments. With nearly seventy figureheads, this museum ranks among the leaders in this area of collecting. From the noble eagle that originally graced the bow of the *Great Republic* to the "noble savage" from the Mystic-built *Seminole*, from carved portraits of specific people like Admiral Farragut from the clipper *Great Admiral* to the ethereal Rhine maiden from the *Rhine*, this collection captures the imagination and diversity of early shipbuilders.

From the extreme of full-sized figureheads, the collection of ship models carries the visitor to the other dimensional extreme. The incredible variety of vessels represented in the more than 600 ship models gives visitors and researchers an exceptional opportunity to study the shape, arrangement, and rigging of many types. Particularly notable are the miniature models built by A. G. Law.

With New England's extensive involvement in the whaling industry, it is logical that one of the most significant collections at Mystic Seaport would be scrimshaw. The range of decorative and utilitarian items produced by whalers in their idle hours is apparent in this collection. Decorated whale teeth or walrus tusks contrast with complex yarn winding swifts or simple whalebone fids. Through it all, a basic artistic merit and sense of design are revealed.

The museum's tool collection is enormous, but the tools of the navigator form an exceptional component. This fine selection of the instruments available to American navigators includes cross-staffs, back staffs, octants, sextants, compasses, chronometers, Gunter's rules, and numerous other instruments and their variations. This collection is of particular interest to researchers.

While the strong, comprehensive collections are at the core of the museum, Mystic Seaport is also distinguished by its staff and its programs. A full offering of educational programs is available from elementary school through undergraduate and graduate level col-

lege work, including courses in everything from navigation to sail education and boatbuilding. The museum publishes both books (with forty titles in print) and videotapes (more than twenty are now available) and supports researchers through its library and manuscript collection and its photographic, film, and video archives. One of the best maritime bookstores in the United States, able to search out and supply books worldwide, is part of the Mystic Seaport Museum Store, as is a gallery that can supply museum-quality models and contemporary maritime art.

In its sixty years, Mystic Seaport Museum has evolved into an effective museum and educational institution. It was not fully planned at its founding, but it responded to opportunities and the perceived needs of those served by the museum. Mystic Seaport has the responsibility to determine what its visitors should learn, and then it strives to make that learning as interesting as possible. While museum visitors experience the past and learn about it painlessly, scholars and researchers painstakingly study the wealth of material collected and preserved at Mystic Seaport Museum. The result, in both instances fulfills the museum's purpose of enhancing knowledge of the sea's influence on American life.

Below: *Figureheads, including* Asia, *in the red turban, the* Rhine, *in green, and* Aleppo, *on the right, stare off into the distance, no longer gracing the bows of ships. (Photo by R. Chalk)*

Above: *Members of the seaport's demonstration squad go aloft to set a sail on the* Joseph Conrad *as one of their numerous daily demonstrations of maritime skills. (Photo by U. Beisler)*

Left: *Interpreter Bill Atkinson demonstrates the use of the forge in the Driggs Shipsmith Shop. (Photo by E. S. French)*

UNITED STATES

THE SAN FRANCISCO MARITIME NATIONAL HISTORICAL PARK, SAN FRANCISCO, CALIFORNIA

by Stephen A. Haller, Curator of Historic Documents

For one hundred years, beginning with the California Gold Rush and continuing through World War II, San Francisco Bay was the most important port on the Pacific shores of both Americas. The San Francisco Maritime National Historical Park exists to preserve the rich maritime heritage of the West Coast, with emphasis on San Francisco Bay and the pivotal role it played in seafaring history in the second half of the 19th century and the first half of the 20th.

At a former ferry terminal at the base of San Francisco's Russian Hill is moored a collection of historic vessels that together represent a major period in the city's maritime heyday. Around the turn of the century, steam was replacing sail, steel hulls were replacing those of wood, and coastal and worldwide trade patterns had been well established. The deep-water and coastal sailing vessels, steam ferries, and tugboats preserved at the museum's Hyde Street Pier give visitors their most dramatic opportunity to feel the deck move beneath their feet, sniff the salt spray, tar, and oil, and experience in some small way the adventure and hard work of the seafaring life. The ships are only the tip of the iceberg, however, the most visually spectacular facet of a comprehensive effort to preserve and display the nation's West Coast maritime heritage.

Adjacent to the vessels floating at the pier is a busy small-craft shop that preserves the working and pleasure craft that complemented the larger vessels and brings to life a once-common waterfront scene. At the far end of a small, sandy beach is the museum's main exhibit building—a streamline-moderne edifice built as a public works project during the Great Depression—housing displays that interpret a wide variety of themes. A little farther down the waterfront are the piers and warehouses of a former U. S. Army Port of Embarkation. Now known as Fort Mason Center, it is the location of the preeminent library of mari-

Opposite: *The bark* Kaiulani *booming through the trades on the way from San Francisco to Durban, South Africa, with a deckload of lumber. This remarkable early color photograph was taken in 1941 by Willard Jorstad, the ship's carpenter. The crew on this voyage included men who would figure prominently in the museum's history—founder Karl Kortum and ship preservationist Harry Dring.*

Above: *Figurehead of the clipper ship* David Crockett, *built at Mystic, Connecticut, in 1853. This piece is one of the museum's most dramatic links with the clipper ship trade in the years during and after the California Gold Rush. It is said that Captain Joseph W. Spencer was so proud of the carving that he had it unshipped for the stormy passage around the Horn and remounted for her entry into San Francisco Bay. (Photo by Steve Danford and Tim Campbell)*

Right: *A Wilhelm Hester photograph of Port Blakely, Washington, in the snow during the winter of 1905. The sailing vessels lined up at the dock are (from left to right,) the four-meter bark* Englehorn, *built in 1889; the four-meter bark* Bracadale, *built in 1887; the three-meter bark* Albania, *built in 1867; the four-meter bark* Wanderer, *built in 1891; the four-meter schooner* Lyman D. Foster, *built in 1892; and the five-meter schooner* Crescent, *built in 1904. The* Wanderer *was the subject of John Masefield's book* The Wanderer of Liverpool. *(Photo by Wilhelm Hester from the Wilhelm Hester Photograph Collection)*

time history on the West Coast, an extensive historic document collection that forms the basis for research, and the storage area for the art and artifacts that have been collected over forty years.

Before the Gold Rush suddenly propelled California into the center of the world stage, the land was the isolated northernmost frontier of Spain's empire in the New World, and about as far from established seaborne trade routes as was possible. It was equally isolated from overland connections by mountains, deserts, and suspicious or hostile native populations when the United States acquired California as a result of war with Mexico in 1846-47.

Within a year, the isolated outpost with a potentially great harbor was transformed into a magnet for migration from all over the world by the discovery of gold on the American River, a tributary of the great inland river system that empties into San Francisco Bay. Thousands of vessels raced to the Golden Gate, carrying fortune seekers fancying themselves new "Argonauts." The shoreline became lined with a "forest of masts," as crews deserted for the diggings. A busy riverboat trade was quickly established to connect the bay with the inland heads of navigation on the Sacramento and San Joaquin rivers. Vessels of all descriptions struggled to windward in order to round stormy Cape Horn and take the shortest route to the gold fields.

Thus, California was flung into the center of worldwide commerce and trade, and the most reliable access for passengers and especially bulky cargo was by sea. This early commerce was of a rather one-sided variety—goods and passengers in, profits out in the form of gold dust. But eventually goldseekers began to settle into more stable pursuits, and agriculture and industry began to develop. Before twenty years had passed, a solid basis for reciprocal trade had been established.

Now iron and steel square-riggers from Europe and wooden down-Easters from the States beat around the Horn with cargoes of coal or general merchandise to exchange for the prodigious grain harvests of California's central valley. Hundreds of vessels arrived each fall in a "second gold rush"—547 in 1881 alone. The incomparable expanses of virgin forest that covered the northwest began to be exploited for railroad ties and building material. Given impetus by railroad expansion, boosted by the need to rebuild after the great San Francisco earthquake of 1906, and sustained by the mushrooming growth of southern California cities in the early 20th century, the lumber industry became a mainstay of West Coast commerce and trade.

Harvesting the vast and untapped food resources of Pacific waters soon began for markets near and far. As Atlantic waters were fished out, and the West Coast was connected with the East by the transcontinental railroad, San Francisco Bay became, for nearly three decades, the center of the whaling industry. The growth of agriculture, fishing, and lumber industries led to development up the Northwest Coast, and because of the rugged terrain and lack of road and rail connections, coastal waters became the major highway, and a busy trade in passengers, lumber, and other goods sprang up. Continuing settlement of Australia,

Above: *This stained-glass window, believed to have once graced the saloon of the Oceanic Steamship Company's passenger steamer* Sonoma, *has been recently restored and now provides a dramatic welcome to visitors at the museum's J. Porter Shaw Library. (Photo by Steve Danford)*

Right: *The* Fort Sutter *was typical of the last generation of riverboats that flourished in the extensive inland waterways leading from San Francisco Bay to the ports of California's great Central Valley. Built in 1914, the* Fort Sutter *ended her days as a beached hulk—one more failed floating restaurant project—only 100 feet from the museum building. This model was built for display at the Panama-Pacific International Exposition of 1915, a "world's fair" that celebrated the completion of the Panama Canal. (Photo by Steve Danford and Tim Campbell)*

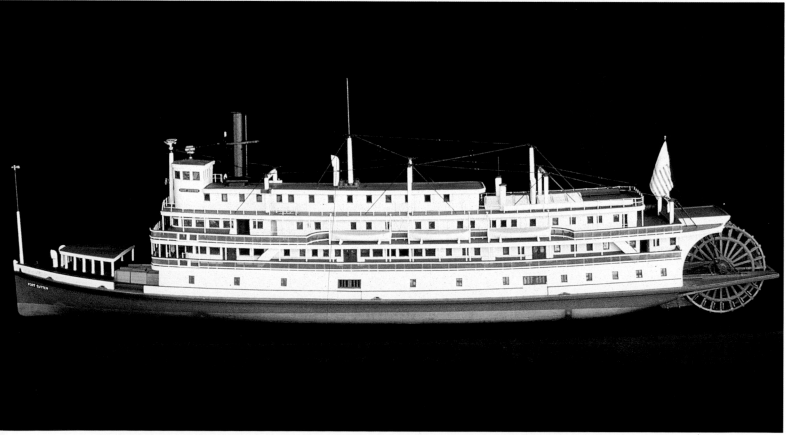

Left: *Captain Schyler Colfax Mitchell (left) was known on the coast as "Crazy" Mitchell for his daring manner of entering port. It would appear that his entire family shared the captain's daring, as they ride the "trapeze chute," used for loading lumber, down to the schooner* Irene, *anchored under the wire at Noyo, California, in 1916.*

Below: *The steamer* Columbia *was knocked off the blocks by the great San Francisco earthquake, while in drydock at the Union Iron Works. The city was burning in the distance when this photograph was taken the next day, April 18, 1906. (Photo from the Bethlehem Shipbuilding Corporation Photograph Collection)*

western expansion of Asian markets, and the importation of "coolie" labor from China and Japan became the foundations upon which a busy transpacific trade developed, pioneered in 1867 by the Pacific Mail Steamship Company. San Francisco also became notable for its early and pivotal role in the fight for sailors' rights and the development of marine labor unionism. In 1934, maritime labor unions began a work stoppage that led to the only successful general strike in the history of the United States.

In the 20th century, the omnipresence of the internal-combustion engine, the discovery of large oil fields in southern California, and the multiplication of the automobile and highways insured that the oil industry and large fleets of tankers would become a mainstay of West Coast commerce. Ironically, this industry also contained some of the seeds of decline for maritime industry on the Pacific shore. The completion of a railroad network and the vast expansion of roads and highway traffic, coincided with the Great Depression and the labor unrest it spawned, to cripple the seagoing trades in the 1930s. World War II brought a great shipbuilding boom to the Bay Area, and San Francisco Bay became the logistical and support center for the Pacific theater of war—and, for a brief period, the nation's busiest port. But the boom of wartime expansion was not maintained in the years of peace that followed.

The ghostly allure of laid-up sailing vessels in "rotten rows" in the bay's backwaters

Above: *Photographer Wilhelm Hester specialized in portraits of vessels and crews at Puget Sound, Washington. This particularly lively image shows the officers and crew of the German three-masted ship* Flottbek *in 1905. Captain Georg Cringler is fourth from left, in the bowler hat. The cook is ready to pour.*

and the memories of wartime service at sea struck a spark of inspiration in a young generation of shipsavers, determined to preserve this rich maritime heritage while remnants still existed and the memories of those who had experienced it were still strong.

In the fall of 1941, the bark *Kaiulani* left San Francisco for what was to be the last commercial rounding of Cape Horn by United States' seamen. The vessel ended her voyage in Australia, where she was converted to a barge. After World War II, some of the younger members of the crew were instrumental in founding a maritime museum in San Francisco. On the nation's eastern seaboard, the National Maritime Historical Society was organized to bring the hull of the *Kaiulani* from the Philippines and restore her as an exhibit in Washington, D. C. Although ultimately unsuccessful, the endeavor of society members contributed to the founding of the South Street Seaport in New York. While only a few scraps of the *Kaiulani* remain at San Francisco, the vessel has inspired two of the country's major maritime museums.

In 1950, a common love of the sea drew together a diverse group of people to found the San Francisco Maritime Museum Association with the goal of establishing a maritime museum in the city. A leading source of the museum vision was Karl Kortum, who grew up on a farm in Petaluma, California, and went to sea on the *Kaiulani*. Local newspapermen Scott Newhall and David Nelson were crucial in fostering public interest and political support for the project. The city granted the association the use of the Aquatic Park Casino, a structure left over from the public works programs of Franklin D. Roosevelt's New Deal, to house a core collection of ship models that had been assembled by Edward S. Clark of the

Pacific Ship Model Society, displayed at the 1939 World's Fair held at Treasure Island in San Francisco, and donated by Alma deBrettville Spreckels, scion of a notable shipping family. Kortum led a crew of volunteers in building exhibits and displays, and the San Francisco Maritime Museum opened its doors in 1951.

The dream that inspired the founders of the museum was saving old ships. In 1954, the derelict hulk of the former British full-rigged ship *Balclutha* was purchased by the Association and pulled off the mudflats of northern San Francisco Bay. An extraordinary year-long cooperative effort followed. Local shipping interests, maritime trade unions, volunteers, seafarers "on the beach," craftsmen, and those with simply a love of the sea worked together and donated time and material to restore the vessel to her appearance in her early days. In 1955, *Balclutha* was opened to the public. Revenues from admission fees allowed the museum to add a small paid staff, including curators Roger Olmstead and Harlan Soeten, to supplement director Karl Kortum. Vessel maintenance, provision for management of the growing collections, exhibits, and the beginning of library services resulted.

The dramatic success of the *Balclutha's* restoration inspired the San Francisco Maritime Museum Association to lobby the state of California to earmark revenue received from the lease of tidelands for oil production for the rescue and acquisition of more historic vessels and their establishment as a maritime state historic park. The steam schooner *Tongass* was saved from retirement in Washington State, partially restored, and rechristened *Wapama;* the three-masted schooner *C. A. Thayer* was rescued from the mudflats of Puget Sound and sailed south; the scow schooner *Alma* was pulled from the shallows of south San

Left: *The lively maritime scene that greets the visitor to the museum's Hyde Street Pier is captured in this 1967 view. At the right is the 1890 sidewheel ferry* Eureka; *in the center is the 1895 coastal lumber schooner C.A. Thayer. The 1915 steam schooner* Wapama, *at the left, has since been moved to the nearby community of Sausalito and placed on a barge in order to preserve her weakened hull. (Photo by Glenn Christiansen, courtesy of Lane Publishing Co.)*

Below: *Two of the museum's distinctly different sailing vessels: the three-masted ship* Balclutha, *built of steel in 1886 near Glasgow, Scotland, and the three-masted schooner C.A. Thayer, built of Douglas fir at Fairhaven, California, in 1895. The felucca* Nuovo Mondo, *a replica of a traditional fishing boat recently built at the museum's Small Craft Shop, floats in the foreground. (Photo by Tim Campbell)*

Above: *The powerful steam tug* Hercules *was built in 1907 for oceangoing towing of ships and log rafts. Later in her career, she pushed barges carrying railroad cars across San Francisco Bay. Seen here at the Hyde Street Pier, her steam plant is presently being restored to full operating condition. (Photo by Richard Frear)*

Francisco Bay; and the paddle ferry *Eureka* joined the fleet straight from the retirement of passenger ferry service on San Francisco Bay. Later, the steam tug *Hercules* was acquired. Restoration work began in Oakland in 1961, under the direction of Harry Dring, who had been prominent in the *Balclutha* effort and had served before the mast on *Kaiulani* with Kortum. Using a former ferry terminal adjacent to the Maritime Museum, the San Francisco Maritime State Historic Park opened to the public in 1963, under Dring's leadership.

In spite of the popularity of their exhibits, upkeep of the ships was a major financial drain for both institutions. In 1972, Congress established the Golden Gate National Recreation Area, and a Congressional staff member and former *Balclutha* volunteer, William G. Thomas, was instrumental in seeing to the inclusion of the historic ships and museum. These institutions joined the National Park Service in 1977 and 1978. On June 27, 1988, Congress created a separate national park composed of the ships and museum and named it the San Francisco Maritime National Historical Park. Shortly thereafter, Thomas, who had joined the Park Service a decade before, became the park's first superintendent.

A great deal of water has passed through the Golden Gate since the Gold Rush, but a bit of 'Frisco's glory days remains along the still-scenic shoreline of San Francisco Bay, and a vital component of the world's maritime heritage is preserved and revered for present and future generations.

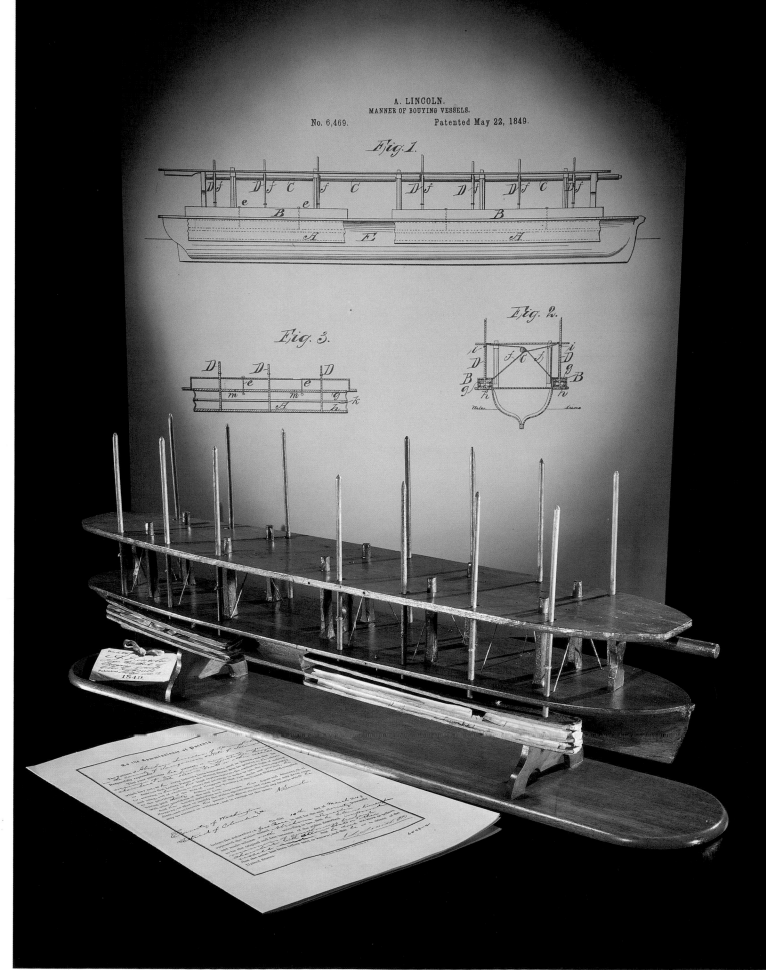

UNITED STATES

THE SMITHSONIAN

INSTITUTION,

WASHINGTON, D.C.

by Paul Forsythe Johnston,
Curator of Maritime History, National
Museum of American History

B ritish scientist James Smithson (1765-1835) never set foot in the United States. Nevertheless, in 1838 this nation became beneficiary to his $515,169 estate "to found at Washington, under the name of the Smithsonian Institution, an establishment for the increase and diffusion of knowledge among men." In this fashion did the world's largest and most heavily visited museum begin; with some additional funding from the U.S. Congress, the doors formally opened to the public in 1855.

The National Watercraft Collection was started by Joseph W. Collins in 1884 as the Section of American Naval Architecture. A former fishing-schooner master from Gloucester, Massachusetts, Captain Collins (1839-1904) had been involved earlier with the U.S. Fish Commission in producing fisheries exhibitions for various world's fairs and international expositions. The ship models displayed at these events, representing the pinnacle of American maritime technological achievement, formed the core of the early Smithsonian nautical collections. By 1923, the holdings had grown in size and scope sufficiently to warrant publication of the National Museum Bulletin 127, *Catalog of the Watercraft Collection.*

Beginning in March 1936, a Works Progress Administration (WPA) project added immensely to the maritime collections by sending dozens of unemployed draftsmen and naval architects around the country to record and collect information on old ships that would otherwise have been lost and forgotten. Although the project was discontinued in October 1937, the plans, models, photographs, and drawings that the workers had gathered expanded the earlier collections significantly. The WPA materials, now collectively known as the Historic American Merchant Marine Survey, were published in 1983 by the Smithsonian Institution. One of the project's regional directors, Howard I. Chapelle, went on to become one of the nation's foremost maritime historians, also serving as the Smithsonian's Curator of Marine Transportation from 1957 to 1967. All of the designs published in his many books,

Opposite: *Abraham Lincoln was the only American president to hold a patent, which he received in 1849 for a new method of altering the draft of vessels for passage through shoal waters in the western rivers. The original patent model was locally made and viewed at least once by Lincoln during his term of office. The original drawings and patent application were stolen from the U. S. Patent Office and never recovered—these copies are among a few sets made and distributed prior to the theft. (Photo by Eric Long)*

Above: *Made in 1813, the Star-Spangled Banner inspired Francis Scott Key to write the national anthem, when he witnessed its raising at Fort McHenry in Baltimore Harbor early on the morning of September 14, 1814. Bearing the 15 stars and stripes authorized by Congress on January 13, 1794, and originally 42 feet long, it was gradually trimmed down to 32 feet by souvenir-hunters. The flag was presented to Lieutenant Colonel George Armistead, the commanding officer of Fort McHenry; his descendants donated it to the Smithsonian in 1912. (Photo by Dane Penland)*

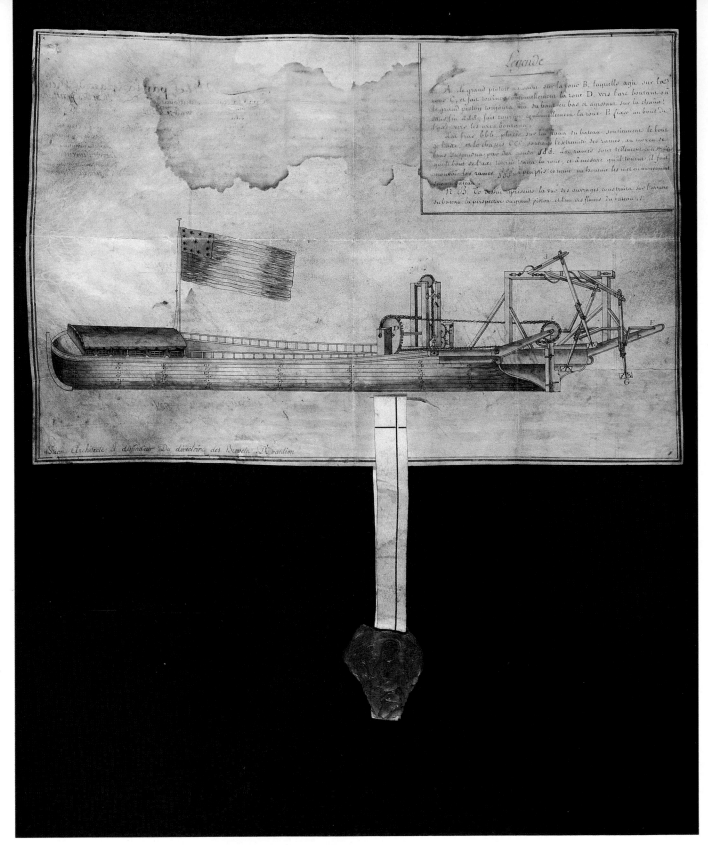

Above: *French patent law had been in effect only 10 months when American inventor John Fitch received this 15-year patent for his steamboat from the French king Louis XVI on November 29, 1791. The reverse of the parchment document (shown) portrays Fitch's invention at an approximate scale of 1/4 inch:1 foot, complete with a* 13-star American flag. The legend describes the steam power plant, chain drive, and stern duck-leg paddles, which move "a little as a man places them in motion on a boat." The obverse permits "John Fitch and his assigns to possess and use fully and peacefully the rights conferred by the presents. . . ." (Photo by Joe A. Goulait)

Left: The gondola Philadelphia, the oldest preserved warship in North America, was part of the "pygmy fleet" of 17 craft constructed at Skenesboro on Lake Champlain (now Whitehall, New York) by Benedict Arnold to counter a newly built British fleet of 53 vessels. The ship was propelled by a single square-rigged mast supplemented by sweeps; the crew totalled around 45 men. Indian sharpshooters along Lake Champlain's shores prevented Philadelphia's crew from going ashore; as a consequence, they lived on board the little warship and ate their meals prepared on the tiny brick hearth amidships. (Photo by Eric Long)

Below: A little of everything—clothing, fishing gear, boats, boat models, dioramas, paintings, sculpture, photographs, and fish—was displayed in the first maritime exhibition produced at a museum in the United States. This photograph of the exhibit, which was mounted at the Smithsonian Castle, dates to the 1880s—only a few years after the building opened to the public.

Above: *On her second voyage, the medium clipper* Coeur de Lion *cleared New York for San Francisco on April 4, 1855. She arrived at the Golden Gate on August 2, together with six other clipper ships from the East Coast, all arriving on the same day. The sight of the seven clippers all together at the wharves was an event never matched. The next leg of Coeur's voyage took 57 days from San Francisco to Hong Kong; it was during the layover at Hong Kong that the Chinese artist Chong Qua painted this portrait. As was common in contemporary clipper ship portraits, the rake of the bow and stern overhang is slightly exaggerated. (Photo by Brenda Gilmore)*

together with thousands of other American ship and boat plans, have been preserved for future generations of boatbuilders and historians, as well as for the public.

Today, the Smithsonian Institution's maritime historical collections are shared among several of the museums on the Mall, with the major concentration in the divisions of Transportation and Armed Forces History at the National Museum of American History (NMAH). These divisions respectively oversee the institutional holdings relating to American maritime enterprise from the origins to the present day: unique as well as commonplace aspects of the story of the nation's waterways, from the inland seas and rivers to the coastal and international offshore waters. The NMAH's exhibits are seen by around six million visitors annually.

The American early struggle for nationhood is perhaps best illustrated by the gunboat *Philadelphia*, which was among a fleet of eight gondolas constructed by Benedict Arnold in 1776 on Lake Champlain, New York, to thwart British encroachment of the northern frontier during the American Revolution. Although *Philadelphia* was sunk in the Battle of Valcour Island, which the British won, the action delayed the English offensive long enough for the rebel Americans to retrench and ultimately obtain French assistance. *Philadelphia* was raised in 1935 and displayed for a quarter century at Lake Champlain before being conserved and transported to the Smithsonian in 1961.

Even more symbolic of the nation's early naval struggle is a torn and fragile remnant of fabric stitched by Mary Pickersgill of Baltimore, Maryland, during the War of 1812. Shortly after the White House was burned in 1814, the British attacked Baltimore. The bombardment of Fort McHenry in Baltimore Harbor was witnessed by a detainee aboard a British ship, who saw the raising of a defiant American flag over the fort at dawn the next morning. The man was Francis Scott Key; the words he penned (set to the melody of an English drinking song) became the national anthem, and Mary Pickersgill's tattered flag, now in the entrance to the National Museum of American History, is the original Star-Spangled Banner.

A spirit of invention and enterprise has always characterized the American people. One of the best-known American steamboat pioneers was the gunsmith and merchant John Fitch (1743-98), who tested his first steamboat on the Delaware River near Philadelphia in 1787. Much of his energy over the next few years was devoted to establishing precedence over his bitter rival James Rumsey, a conflict essential to obtaining exclusive steamboat patents and attracting financial backers. Both inventors traveled to Europe to raise funds for their projects, and while in France, Fitch was granted a patent for his duck-leg paddle steamer on November 29, 1791, by King Louis XVI.

At around the same time, Colonel John Stevens (1749-1838) of New Jersey began experimenting with steamboats, testing hydraulic jets and sidewheel paddles before finally settling on screw propulsion. In 1803-4, he built the twin-screw steamer *Little Juliana*, which reached a speed of four miles per hour in New York Harbor. Although the hull was later lost, the powerplant was preserved and exhibited at the World's Columbian Exposition of 1892 before being added to the National Watercraft Collection.

Opposite, bottom: *In 1847, the U. S. Congress passed legislation subsidizing an American transatlantic steamship service, in an effort to compete with the British Cunard Line. The contract was won by Edward Knight Collins (1802–78). In 1850, four Collins liners inaugurated service as the fastest and most lavishly fitted-out steamships in the world. This 1851 oil painting by L. H. F. Gamain depicts the Collins liner* Atlantic *entering Liverpool harbor; the British vessels have canted their yards as a symbol of mourning for the loss of the transatlantic speed record. The loss at sea of two of the four Collins steamships in 1854 and 1856 proved devastating to the line's reputation; despite the construction of a fifth ship in 1857, the firm foundered in February 1858. (Photo by Kim Nelson)*

Following pages: *Few things were more distasteful to the officers of merchant sailing vessels than seeing sailors sitting about idly with nothing to do. However, whaleships were different in this respect, since a single voyage might last four years and there were long periods of enforced idleness when the ships slowly cruised the hunting grounds searching for their prey. One of the ways sailors on whalers occupied their free time was by carving whales' teeth, bone, and baleen with ornamental designs, known as scrimshaw. Traditionally, it was given to friends, family, or loved ones as souvenirs once the sailor returned home. (Photo by Eric Long)*

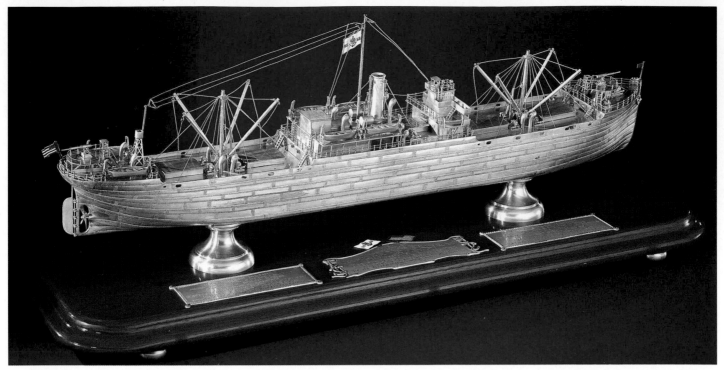

Even Abraham Lincoln caught the fever of maritime innovation. On May 22, 1849, he was granted U.S. Patent No. 6,469 for his invention of "a new and improved manner of combining adjustable buoyant air chambers with steam boats . . . for the purpose of enabling their draught of water to be readily lessened." A glance at his original patent model, one of around 10,000 at the NMAH, will readily show that Lincoln's considerable talents lay elsewhere; nevertheless, he remains the only American president ever granted a patent.

Around the time Lincoln was experimenting with navigation, the entire nation was learning about a new maritime venture resulting from the discovery of gold in California. The prospect of instant riches was too powerful to resist, and Easteners were anxious to try their luck in the California goldfields. In the late 1840s, the clipper ship was just beginning to achieve prominence as the fastest type of ship for the China trade, and it was pressed into service for voyages around Cape Horn at the southern tip of South America—some of the most dangerous and demanding waters in the world. From the start, the California clippers were associated with great speed, which they achieved through a combination of extra sail coverage and long, narrow hulls. Although the clipper era lasted only a decade or so, it left an indelible impression on the American mind.

Coeur de Lion, a medium clipper built in 1854 at Portsmouth, New Hampshire, was a late and fairly typical example of the class. Although she never set any speed records, she served a number of owners well in the California and China trades before her sale to foreign owners in 1860. Normally, the useful life of an American clipper was only about a decade because of hard-use in unforgiving waters, but *Coeur de Lion* lived to the age of sixty-one before wrecking in the Baltic in August 1915, victim of a collision.

One of the reasons for the short life of the American clipper was the financial depression of 1857, which cut shipbuilding activity along the East Coast to almost nothing. The Civil War also seriously curtailed American deepwater commerce, for insurance rates skyrocketed during wartime and many shipowners were forced to sell their fleets to foreign

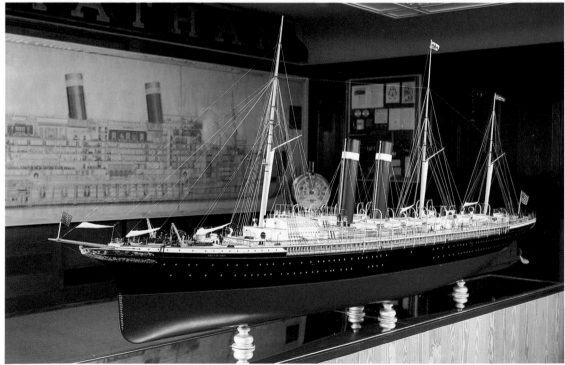

Left: *The ocean liner* Philadelphia *was truly an international ship. When built at Glasgow in 1888–89 as* City of Paris, *she and her sister ship* New York *were the largest ships in the world. When the American Line was established in 1893, both vessels transferred to American registry; with the outbreak of the Spanish-American War in 1898,* Paris *was renamed* Yale *and served as an auxiliary scouting cruiser. After the war and another new name,* Philadelphia *returned to transatlantic service until World War I, when the U. S. Navy requisitioned her again for troop transport service to France as* Harrisburg. *In 1919, she returned to the American Line renamed* Philadelphia, *but was bought by an Italian line in 1923 for the transport of immigrants. While in Naples, the crew mutinied and set the ship on fire; she drifted ashore and was finally broken up in 1925. (Photo by Kim Nielsen)*

owners. And when the war ended, naval sailing ships were obsolete, superseded by steam-powered ironclads.

Aside from the ironclad, one of the few types of shipping that emerged and thrived during the Civil War was the Confederate blockade runner; around 200 of these "gray ghosts" were special-built to slip through the Union blockade of the Confederate ports. One of the most extreme examples of the class was *Presto* (ex-*Fergus*), launched in the middle of the night of August 1, 1863, at Glasgow, Scotland, by the famous clipper builders Alexander Stephens & Sons. Most merchant vessels of the time were three to four times longer than they were wide; an extreme clipper might have a 4-5:1 length:beam ratio. Built lightly for speed at a ratio of 10:1, *Presto* reached twenty and one-half knots during trials. Painted gray and riding low in the water to escape detection, she made two successful and highly profitable runs through the federal blockade before going aground at Fort Moultrie off Charleston, South Carolina, on February 2, 1864. Union batteries destroyed her almost immediately.

After the Civil War, American deepwater shipping went into a steep decline from which it never fully recovered. Hundreds of ships were lost, sold, or transferred to foreign flags during the war, and special interest groups conspired to prevent their reregistration under the American flag. Postwar shortages in skilled shipyard laborers drove up shipbuilding costs, and the British took over disrupted American trade patterns while also surpassing the United States in the transition from wooden to iron shipbuilding. The "iron horse," or railroad, also was an important factor in the decline of transcontinental shipping, as the nation began looking inward during Reconstruction. In fact, aside from increased activity during this century's world wars, the American merchant marine is, quite literally, history—not a single deepwater merchant ship is under construction in the United States today.

However, shipbuilding and commerce remained vital on the inland waterways—the Mississippi River system and the Great Lakes—and these waters are still essential today to the transport of large bulk cargoes. Some of the most famous American ship types were developed for these waterways and the deepwater trades last century, as immortalized in the works of authors Herman Melville, Mark Twain, Richard Henry Dana, and Rudyard Kipling. The Mississippi sternwheel riverboat and clipper ship are images as enduring as the cowboy in America's heritage; the Great Lakes whaleback is an unmatched embodiment of Alexis de Tocqueville's characterization of the American people as "enterprising, fond of adventure, and, above all, of novelty." Americans tend to forget that the great coasting schooners, with as many as seven masts, were once as important to the nation's commerce as trailer trucks are today. With these huge multi-masters, working sail made its last stand in America's home waters—yet none has been preserved in working condition. Likewise, regional small craft with such evocative names as moses boats, cowhorns, melon seeds, flatties, pinkies, skipjacks, peapods, dinks, dories, and duckers are preserved all too often only in plans or reproductions. In collecting for the nation, the Smithsonian Institution preserves representative expressions of the full range of America's maritime ancestry, and the lives of the people who created and sustained that initiative.

Opposite, top: *This engine room is one of the centerpieces in the Smithsonian's Hall of American Maritime Enterprise. The triple-expansion steam engine was built in 1920 by the John W. Sullivan Machine Company of New York. Rated at 750 horsepower, in 1921 it was installed in the U. S. Coast Guard cutter* Oak, *which served for 50 years as a buoy tender in Chesapeake Bay. Beginning in the 1930s, diesel engines superseded steam power plants in most coastal and inland seas ships. (Photo by Kim Nielsen)*

Opposite, bottom: *Complete with a sound track of contemporary operative communications equipment, this exhibit gallery in the Hall of American Maritime Enterprise recreates the radio room of a merchant vessel of the early 1920s. Included are a 500-watt panel radio set, a medium-wave receiver, an auxiliary hand sending key, and a two-step amplifier. (Photo by Kim Nielsen)*

UNITED STATES

THE SOUTH STREET SEAPORT

MUSEUM, NEW YORK,

NEW YORK

by Peter Neill, President

M ore than a haven, more than a harbor, a port is a place of exchange—of goods, people, and ideas. While the history of each of the world's great ports is individual and specific, their anatomy and evolution is astonishingly similar. The port of New York is a preeminent example, and its story defines the purpose of the South Street Seaport Museum.

How was a naturally advantageous network of waterways found, made, used, and abused by generations from worlds old and new, east and west? How did a tiny imperial trading post ultimately become a center of global commerce and culture? How did maritime endeavor transform an aboriginal settlement into a cosmopolitan center and contemporary metropolis?

The answers to these questions are found in the social history of New York: in the work of the laborers, artisans, and merchants who made the port, built the city, and profited more or less from its prosperity; in the commerce that made the city renowned, the destination of countless ships, and the focal point of transoceanic trade; and in the many and varied communities of people from foreign lands who contributed to the vital collective culture of the city we know today.

The centerpiece of the museum's collection, then, is the port itself—its natural beauty, its changing activity, its historical meaning—and we have elected to interpret this irreplacable artifact on a massive scale.

How? Through excursion vessels that take more than 300,000 passengers each year on informative harbor history tours. Through buildings: twelve blocks of 19th-century waterfront structures, restored and converted to museum, restaurant, and retail use. Through ships: a fleet that includes the four-masted bark *Peking* (1911), the full-rigged ship *Wavertree* (1885), the lightship *Ambrose* (1908), the steam ferry *General William H. Hart* (1925), the tugboat *W. O. Decker* (1930), and the two operating schooners *Pioneer* (1885)

Opposite: *The masts of the 1911 bark* Peking *tower above the roof of Schermerhorn Row, an 1811 commercial building in which the South Street Seaport Museum's permanent exhibit on the history of the Port of New York will be housed.*

Following pages: *The century-old coasting schooner* Pioneer *sails past the Statue of Liberty with a "cargo" of museum passengers. She is an excellent example of how working historic vessels can augment museum programs while earning their costs of operation and repair.*

and *Lettie G. Howard* (1893). Through programs: an ambitious schedule of changing exhibits, educational services, maritime events, festivals, and outdoor concerts that make the museum an imaginative contributor to the experience of the modern city.

    The South Street Seaport Museum was founded in 1968 by a group of volunteers dedicated to the reclamation of the abandoned East River waterfront historically known as "the street of ships," those piers south of the Brooklyn Bridge where had docked the first packet ships to England and the continent, the first clipper ships bound for Far Eastern markets, the first coastwise schooners that had linked New York southward to the West Indies, northward to Maine and the Maritimes, and the first canal boats that had opened interior trade to the Great Lakes and beyond through the Erie Canal. Our piers were a confusion of maritime enterprise, a phenomenon suggested again in 1986 when New York and South Street celebrated the Statue of Liberty Centennial with "Operation Sail," a gathering of "tall ships" of twenty-three nations on parade down the harbor, an event witnessed by a spectator fleet of more than 40,000 vessels. Fifteen historic ships docked at the museum; some 350,000 people visited the piers over three days.

Below: *The 1908 lightship* Ambrose, *once guardian of the entrance to New York harbor, is now moored at the Museum Pier 16 and is open to the public.*

Left: *The Fulton Fish Market, the largest such market in the United States, is an authentic and lively vestige of 19th-century commerce. The market operates through the night in the streets of the Seaport historic district, providing a 24-hour "exhibit" of colorful maritime tradition.*

Below: *The* Peking *in drydock for refurbishment of her hull, a magnificent sight and significant achievement in the museum's ambitious program of maintenance and restoration of its fleet of historic ships.*

If the buildings were derelict, the Fulton Fish Market was alive and well with its 19th-century appearance remarkably intact. Today, the wholesalers and loaders still conduct their business through the night by the light of open fires, the fish arrayed for buyers from throughout the region. The museum, as landlord to the market, has the privilege of preserving an authentic, living artifact that retains all the color, frenetic movement, and individualistic behavior of the past.

The museum slowly assembled rights to various buildings in the district, including Schermerhorn Row, built in 1812 by Peter Schermerhorn, a merchant and one of New York's first real estate entrepreneurs. With comparable spirit, the founders pursued a dream of a unique partnership of culture and commerce, public and private, profit and nonprofit entities that, together, could meet the extraordinary financial challenge of rebuilding the physical and spiritual identity of the neighborhood. In collaboration with the city, the state of New York, and federal government grant programs for urban redevelopment, major improvements to buildings, streets, and piers were accomplished. In cooperation with The Rouse

Below: Castle Garden, New York, *by Edward Moran (1829-1901), depicts the diversity of vessels typical of New York harbor in the 19th century.*

Company, real estate developers who had undertaken dramatic projects in Boston, Massachusetts, and Baltimore, Maryland, more than 270,000 square feet of restaurant and retail space was completed in existing structures or new construction. A historic district was established and extended to encompass the largest concentration remaining of the city's earliest architecture. In 1978, the museum assumed the responsibility for a ninety-nine-year city lease for the district and created its own nonprofit development corporation to oversee The Rouse Company, additional office and residential tenants, and a new 250-room hotel. In 1989, the project produced more than 2,500 jobs, $100 million in sales, and $16 million in city and state taxes. By 1992, total investment in the area will exceed $500 million, resulting in a major waterfront renewal, a significant tourist attraction, a highly visible, financially successful public development achievement, and an amenity that sustains civility in an otherwise chaotic urban environment.

In 1985, the museum embarked on additional expansion by renovating the A. A. Low Building to include two floors of temporary exhibit space. Low and his brothers were early

The Andrew Fletcher, *a replica of a 19th-century double sidewheeler, is seen against the backdrop of the modern city. The Seaport Line fleet takes over 300,000 passengers a year on tours of the harbor and includes a second replica boat and the* Honey Fitz, *official yacht of John F. Kennedy and five other American presidents.*

merchant bankers and owned a fleet of clipper ships that departed South Street for record-breaking passages to China and Japan, bringing back to New York cargoes of tea, silks, and porcelains. Recently, the top three floors of their brownstone counting house were transformed into a state-of-the-art storage facility for the museum's artifact collection and a bridge was built to connect the Low Building to the upper floors of Schermerhorn Row, wherein a 20,000-square-foot permanent exhibit on the port of New York is being installed.

Beyond ships and buildings, the South Street collection necessarily centers around items related to New York maritime history: paintings, prints, drawings, photographs, models, and ephemera. The museum mounts eight changing exhibits a year in four galleries on such subjects as New York shipbuilding, international trade, ocean liners, port navigation, and immigration. In addition, the museum has had a long interest in the history of printing, accumulating one of the finest collections of antique presses and 19th-century display and montotype in the United States. "Bowne and Company, Printers" is a recreated job printing establishment that utilizes the collections for instructional programs and offers products for sale, including limited-edition publications. In 1988, the museum also accepted over 1 million objects excavated from construction sites in lower Manhattan, thereby acquiring significant amounts of colonial period artifacts and becoming a national center for urban archaeology. In 1990, in order to expose this material to the public, the museum opened a satellite center containing archaeological exhibits, a conservation laboratory, and audio- visual and educational space.

Education is the museum's major purpose. Every visitor is offered a tour led by a member of the education staff of thirty full-time interpreters, which is supplemented by a growing group of trained volunteers. Through an innovative adopt-a-school program, the education staff cooperates with elementary school teachers to develop and test curricula devoted to New York City history. More than 42,500 students participate annually in educational programs specifically created by the museum for delivery on-site and in schools. In addition, the museum publishes *Seaport*, an illustrated quarterly devoted to all aspects of New York history and distributed to 10,000 subscribers. Two lecture series are presented annually, and courses are offered in maritime skills, particularly small craft construction, in the museum Boatbuilding Shop. A constant stream of visiting historic vessels offers continuing possibilities for special programs, and the museum's annual Wooden Boat Festival and Schooner Race, evocative manifestations of a renaissance of interest in things maritime, draw thousands of additional visitors to our piers.

In effect, the South Street Seaport Museum is a "museum without walls," serving an audience of millions. It is experience as diverse in the present as seaport life was in the past. It involves both tourist and scholar in search of history. It involves the downtown worker in search of recreation and entertainment. It involves the city dweller in search of fulfilled communal needs. In each case, there is an exchange—of goods, people, ideas—in a place that demonstrates like no other the historical meaning and contemporary value of American maritime heritage.

Above: *Murray Cukier, model maker and folk artist, is one of numerous participants in "Maritime New York," a summer-long festival of contemporary marine arts and crafts sponsored by the museum.*

Above: *L.A. Briggs (1852-1931) portrait of the* Yorkshire, *one of the Black Bell Line ships that originated regularly scheduled packet service between Liverpool and New York.*

Left: *These examples of British earthenware are representative of the museum's inventory of more than a million pieces of archaeological material excavated from various sites in lower Manhattan.*

INDEX

The names of ships are italicized. Also italicized: page numbers indicating illustrations of ships and works by the artist cited.)